ECO HOUSES

ECO-HÄUSER

HABITAT RÉSIDENTIAL ÉCOLOGIQUE

EXCLUSIEVE ECO-WONINGEN

CASAS ECOLÓGICAS

ABITAZIONI ECOSOSTENIBILI

ECO-HABITAÇÕES RESIDENCIAIS

KÖNEMANN
is an imprint of
Frechmann Kolón GmbH
www.frechmann.com

© 2014 for this edition: Frechmann Kolón GmbH

Editorial project:
LOFT Publications
Barcelona, Spain
Tel.: +34 932 688 088
Fax: +34 932 687 073
loft@loftpublications.com
www.loftpublications.com

Editorial coordinator:
Simone K. Schleifer

Assistant to editorial coordination:
Aitana Lleonart Triquell

Editor:
Cristina Paredes Benítez

Art director:
Mireia Casanovas Soley

Design and layout coordination:
Claudia Martínez Alonso

Layout:
MH

Translations:
Cillero & de Motta
Mengès (FR)

Published in the United States in 2015 by:

Skyhorse Publishing
307 West 36th Street, 11th Floor
New York, NY 10018, USA
T: +1 212 643 6816
info@skyhorsepublishing.com
www.skyhorsepublishing.com

978-3-86407-342-7 (GB)
978-3-86407-340-3 (D)
978-3-86407-343-4 (NL)
978-3-86407-341-0 (E)
978-3-86407-344-1 (PORT)
978-1-63220-595-7 (Skyhorse, USA)

Printed in Spain

1. CONCEPTS

Concepts such as carbon footprints, passive systems, bioclimatic housing, ecological certification, photovoltaic panels or natural materials are common, but what does each term mean? The main ones are outlined below.

1. KONZEPTE

Konzepte wie ökologischer Fußabdruck, passive Systeme, bioklimatische Häuser, Umweltzertifizierungen, Fotovoltaikpaneele oder natürliches Baumaterial sind inzwischen schon geläufig - aber was bedeuten sie im Einzelnen? Im Folgenden wird versucht, die wichtigsten dieser Konzepte zu erläutern.

1. NOUVEAUX CONCEPTS

Des expressions comme empreinte écologique, installations passives, logements bioclimatiques, labels écologiques, panneaux photovoltaïques ou matériaux naturels font partie de notre quotidien, mais savons-nous vraiment ce que signifient tous ces termes ? Voici, en quelques lignes, des définitions et explications claires.

1. BEGRIPPEN

Ecologische voetafdruk, passieve systemen, bioklimatische woning, milieucertificaten, zonnepanelen of natuurlijke materialen zijn alledaagse begrippen, maar wat betekenen deze termen nu eigenlijk? Op deze bladzijden wordt geprobeerd om de belangrijkste begrippen uit te leggen.

1. CONCEPTOS

Conceptos como huella ecológica, sistemas pasivos, vivienda bioclimática, certificaciones ecológicas, paneles fotovoltaicos o materiales naturales ya son habituales pero, ¿qué significa cada uno de estos términos? En estas líneas se explican los más relevantes.

1. CONCETTI

Concetti quali impronta ecologica, sistemi passivi, abitazione bioclimatica, certificazioni ecologiche, pannelli fotovoltaici o materiali naturali sono ormai abituali, ma qual è il significato di ciascuno di questi termini? In queste righe si cercherà di spiegare il significato dei più rilevanti.

1. CONCEITOS

Conceitos como pegada ecológica, sistemas passivos, habitação bioclimática, certificações ecológicas, painéis fotovoltaicos ou materiais naturais já são habituais, mas o que significa cada um destes termos? Nestas linhas tentam-se explicar os mais relevantes.

© Garrison Architects   * 1.1

1.1. Carbon footprint

Carbon footprinting measures how much land and water are required by a population to produce the resources it consumes and to absorb the waste using current technology. Ideally, all areas of life should not consume more resources than those which Nature can regenerate. For housing, the carbon footprint adds up the CO_2 emitted during construction (the transport of materials and workers for its duration), the source of the materials and the energy needed for its workings.
Prefabricated housing reduces the carbon footprint as construction time is lessened as are the CO_2 emissions for transportation of materials and workers.

1.1. Ökologischer Fußabdruck

Der ökologische Fußabdruck misst, wie viel Land und Wasser ein Ort benötigt, um die Ressourcen, die er verbraucht, zu erzeugen und die Abfälle zu absorbieren, indem er die vorhandene Technologie nutzt. Der Idealfall ist, wenn alle Lebensbereiche nur die Ressourcen verbrauchen, die von der Natur auch regeneriert werden können. Bei Häusern müsste man für den ökologischen Fußabdruck das während des Baus abgegebene CO_2 (beim Material- und Mitarbeitertransport während des Baus), die Herkunft des Baumaterials oder die für ihr Funktionieren notwendige Energie zusammenrechnen.
Bei Fertighäusern senkt sich der ökologische Fußabdruck, da die Bauzeit kürzer ist und die CO_2-Abgaben beim Material- und Mitarbeitertransport geringer sind.

1.1. Empreinte écologique

L'empreinte écologique mesure la quantité de terres et d'eau nécessaire à une population pour produire les ressources qu'elle consomme et absorber les rejets à l'aide des technologies existantes. Dans l'idéal, il ne faudrait en aucune circonstance consommer plus de ressources que la nature n'est capable de régénérer. L'empreinte écologique d'un logement prend en compte le CO_2 produit pendant sa construction (acheminement des matériaux et des ouvriers sur le chantier), l'origine des matériaux et l'énergie nécessaire à son fonctionnement.

L'empreinte écologique des logements préfabriqués est moindre puisque la durée de construction et les émissions de CO_2 résultant du transport de matériaux et des ouvriers sont plus courtes.

1.1. Ecologische voetafdruk

De ecologische voetafdruk meet hoeveel grond- en wateroppervlakte een bevolkingsgroep nodig heeft om de middelen die hij consumeert te produceren en zijn afvalproductie te kunnen verwerken met behulp van de bestaande technologie. Ideaal zou zijn dat er niet meer middelen worden geconsumeerd dan die de natuur kan produceren. In woningen wordt de ecologische voetafdruk bepaald door de tijdens de bouw uitgestoten CO_2 (transport van materialen en arbeiders), de oorsprong van de materialen of de energie die voor het functioneren van het huis nodig is.

Prefab woningen verlagen de ecologische voetafdruk aangezien de bouwtijd gereduceerd en de CO_2-uitstoot bij het vervoer van materialen en arbeiders verminderd wordt.

1.1. Huella ecológica

La huella ecológica mide cuánta superficie de tierra y agua requiere una población para producir los recursos que consume y absorber los desechos usando la tecnología existente. Lo ideal es que en todos los ámbitos de la vida no se consuman más recursos que los que la naturaleza puede regenerar. En las viviendas, la huella ecológica sumaría el CO_2 emitido durante la construcción (transporte de materiales y trabajadores durante la edificación), la producción o extracción de los materiales o la energía necesaria para su funcionamiento.

Las viviendas prefabricadas reducen la huella ecológica al reducir el tiempo de construcción y las emisiones de CO_2 derivadas del transporte de materiales y trabajadores.

1.1. Impronta ecologica

L'impronta ecologica misura la porzione di territorio (sia esso terra o acqua) di cui una popolazione necessita per produrre le risorse che consuma ed assorbire i rifiuti usando la tecnologia esistente. L'ideale è che in tutti gli ambiti della vita non si consumino più risorse di quelle che la natura è in grado di rigenerare. Nelle abitazioni, l'impronta ecologica deve tenere conto del CO_2 emesso durante la costruzione (trasporto di materiali e dipendenti durante l'edificazione), l'origine dei materiali o l'energia necessaria per il suo funzionamento.

Le abitazioni prefabbricate riducono l'impronta ecologica in quanto necessitano tempi di costruzione inferiori che comportano una riduzione delle emissioni di CO_2 per il trasporto dei materiali e dei dipendenti.

1.1. Pegada ecológica

A pegada ecológica mede a área de terra e de água que uma população requer para produzir os recursos que consome e absorver os desperdícios usando a tecnologia existente. O ideal é que em todos os âmbitos da vida não se consumam mais recursos que os que a natureza pode regenerar. Nas habitações, a pegada ecológica soma o CO_2 emitido durante a construção (transporte de materiais e trabalhadores durante a edificação), a origem dos materiais ou a energia necessária para o seu funcionamento.

As habitações pré-fabricadas reduzem a pegada ecológica ao reduzir o tempo de construção e as emissões de CO_2 do transporte de materiais e trabalhadores.

*1.2

1.2. Certifications

Over the past few years a number of certifications calculating the energy efficiency of buildings have been developed. Some of these are used as international benchmarks, such as LEED (Leadership in Energy & Environmental Design) from the USA or Passiv Haus from Germany. The former is a framework which determines the use of sustainable construction strategies, from air quality to alternative energies while the Passiv Haus certification calculates the use of passive measures to heat and air-condition buildings.

Studio 804 has based the design of this home on standards required by the LEED certification. The house uses geothermal and aeolian energy and collects rainwater.

1.2. Zertifizierungen

In den letzten Jahren wurden verschiedene Zertifizierungen zur Berechnung der Energieeffizienz der Gebäude geschaffen. Einige darunter wie LEED (Leadership in Energy & Enviromental Design) in den USA oder die deutsche Passivhaus-Zertifizierung werden als internationale Standards eingesetzt. Bei der Erstgenannten handelt es sich um ein Regelwerk für den Einsatz nachhaltiger Baustrategien, die von der Luftqualität bis zu alternativen Energien reichen. Das Passivhaus-Zertifikat misst den Einsatz passiver Maßnahmen bei der Gebäudeklimatisierung.

Studio 804 basiert das Design dieser Wohnung auf die von der LEED-Zertifizierung geforderten Standards. Das Haus wird mit Erdwärme und Windenergie versorgt und fängt das Regenwasser auf.

1.2. Écolabels

Ces dernières années ont vu naître plusieurs labels qui indiquent l'efficacité énergétique des bâtiments. Certains sont aujourd'hui des standards internationaux, comme la certification délivrée par LEED (Leadership in Energy & Environmental Design) aux États-Unis ou Passivhaus en Allemagne. Le premier est un ensemble de normes qui définit l'emploi de stratégies de construction respectueuses de l'environnement, de la qualité de l'air à l'emploi d'énergies alternatives. Le label Passivhaus, lui, récompense l'emploi de mesures passives pour chauffer ou climatiser un bâtiment.

Studio 804 a conçu les plans de cette résidence en respectant le cahier des charges défini pour l'obtention du label LEED. La maison produit son énergie en associant géothermie et éoliennes. Les eaux pluviales sont collectées.

1.2. Certificaten

De laatste jaren zijn diverse certificaten gecreëerd die de energie-efficiëntie van gebouwen berekenen. Sommige worden gebruikt als internationale standaarden, zoals het LEED (Leadership in Energy & Enviromental Design) in de VS of het Duitse Passiv Haus. Het eerste is een normensysteem dat het gebruik van duurzame bouwstrategieën regelt, van de luchtkwaliteit tot alternatieve energieën. Het Passiv Haus-certificaat meet het gebruik van passieve maatregelen om een gebouw te verwarmen/koelen.

Studio 804 baseert het ontwerp van deze woning op de door het LEED-systeem gestelde eisen. Het huis wordt voorzien van geothermische energie, windenergie en een regenwateropvangsysteem.

1.2. Certificaciones

En los últimos años se han creado varias certificaciones que calculan la eficiencia energética de los edificios. Algunas de ellas se utilizan como estándares internacionales, como la LEED (Leadership in Energy & Enviromental Design) en EE. UU. o la alemana Passiv Haus. La primera es un sistema de normas que rige el uso de estrategias constructivas sostenibles, desde la calidad del aire hasta las energías alternativas. El certificado Passiv Haus mide el uso de medidas pasivas para climatizar un edificio.

Studio 804 ha diseñado esta residencia según los estándares que exige la certificación LEED. La casa utiliza energía geotérmica, energía eólica y un sistema de recogida de aguas pluviales.

1.2. Certificazioni

In questi ultimi anni sono state sviluppate varie certificazioni che calcolano l'efficacia energetica degli edifici. Alcune di esse sono state adottate come standard internazionali, come ad esempio la LEED (Leadership in Energy & Enviromental Design) negli USA o la tedesca Passiv Haus. La prima rappresenta un sistema di norme che disciplina l'uso delle strategie costruttive sostenibili, dalla qualità dell'aria alle energie alternative. Il certificato Passiv Haus misura l'adozione di strategie passive per la climatizzazione di un edificio.

Studio 804 basa il progetto di questa residenza sugli standard esigiti dalla certificazione LEED. La casa si rifornisce d'energia geotermica ed eolica ed è dotata di un sistema di raccolta delle acque piovane.

1.2. Certificações

Nos últimos anos foram criadas várias certificações que calculam a eficiência energética dos edifícios. Algumas delas são utilizadas como padrões internacionais, como a LEED (Leadership in Energy & Enviromental Design) nos EUA ou a alemã Passivhaus. A primeira é um sistema de normas que rege o uso de estratégias construtivas sustentáveis, desde a qualidade do ar até às energias alternativas. O certificado Passivhaus mede o uso de medidas passivas para climatizar um edifício.

O Studio 804 baseia a concepção desta residência nos padrões que a certificação LEED exige. A casa contempla a utilização de energia geotérmica, de energia eólica e a recolha de águas pluviais.

1.3. Energy efficiency

Defined as a reduction in energy consumption while maintaining services or levels of comfort and quality of life. It is applied to all aspects of our lives: to electrical appliances, housing and transport. If electrical appliances over ten years old were replaced with class A ones, consumption of electricity would be reduced as would the resulting CO_2 emissions from the burning of fossil fuels. Replacing incandescent light bulbs with low consumption LEDs also contributes to a home's energy efficiency.

This image shows energy classification, be it that of an electrical appliance or a house. It is usually applied to the kWh consumption of each element.

* 1.3

1.3. Energieeffizienz

Sie wird als Senkung des Energieverbrauchs definiert, während die Serviceleistungen, Komfortansprüche und Lebensqualität erhalten bleiben. Sie findet auf alle Lebensbereiche wie Hausgeräte, Wohnung oder Transport Anwendung. Durch den Austausch der über 10 Jahre alten Hausgeräte gegen Klasse-A-Hausgeräte, könnten der Stromverbrauch und damit die aus der Verbrennung fossiler Brennstoffe entstehenden CO_2-Abgaben gesenkt werden. Das Auswechseln der Glühbirnen gegen Glühbirnen mit niedrigem Verbrauch oder LED-Lampen trägt auch zur Energieeffizienz eines Hauses bei.

Auf dem Bild ist die Energieeinstufung eines Hausgeräts oder eines ganzen Hauses dargestellt. Normalerweise gilt sie für den kWh-Verbrauch der einzelnen Teile.

1.3. Efficacité énergétique

Elle mesure la réduction de la consommation d'énergie à confort et qualité de vie égaux. Ce calcul peut être appliqué à tous les aspects de notre quotidien : aux appareils électroménagers, au logement ou au transport. Si l'on renouvelait tous les appareils électroménagers de plus de dix ans par d'autres de classe A, la consommation d'électricité diminuerait, entraînant donc une baisse des émissions de CO_2 résultant de l'emploi de combustibles fossiles. Remplacer les ampoules incandescentes par des modèles basse consommation ou à leds améliore également l'efficacité énergétique d'une maison.

L'étiquette indique le bilan énergie, qu'il s'agisse de l'électroménager ou d'une maison. Normalement, elle indique la consommation en kWh de chaque appareil.

1.3. Energie-efficiëntie

Energie-efficiëntie wordt omschreven als de vermindering van het energieverbruik zonder aan de comfort- en levenskwaliteitsstandaarden in te boeten. Het wordt op elk aspect van ons leven toegepast: op huishoudelijke apparatuur, de woning of het transport. Worden huishoudelijke apparaten die ouder dan 10 jaar zijn voor andere van klasse A vervangen, dan wordt het stroomverbruik en dus de resulterende CO_2-uitstoot van de verbranding van fossiele brandstoffen gereduceerd. Worden gloeilampen voor spaarlampen of ledden vervangen, dan wordt ook bijgedragen aan de energie-efficiëntie in huis.

De afbeelding toont de energieclassificatie, hetzij van een huishoudelijk apparaat hetzij van een huis. Gewoonlijk wordt deze toegepast op het verbruik van kWh per element.

1.3. Eficiencia energética

Se define como la reducción del consumo de energía manteniendo los servicios o estándares de confort y calidad de vida. Se aplica a cualquier aspecto de nuestra vida: a los electrodomésticos, la vivienda o al transporte. Si se cambiaran los electrodomésticos de más de diez años por otros de clase A se reduciría el consumo eléctrico y, por tanto, las emisiones de CO_2 resultantes de la quema de combustibles fósiles. El cambiar las bombillas incandescentes por otras de bajo consumo o leds también contribuye a la eficiencia energética de la casa.

La imagen muestra la clasificación energética, ya sea de un electrodoméstico o de una casa. Normalmente se aplica al consumo de kWh de cada elemento.

1.3. Efficienza energetica

Viene definita come l'insieme delle azioni che permettono la riduzione del consumo energetico mantenendo i servizi o gli standard di comfort e qualità di vita. È applicata a qualunque aspetto della nostra vita: agli elettrodomestici, all'abitazione o al trasporto. Ad esempio, sostituendo gli elettrodomestici che hanno più di 10 anni di vita con altri di classe A, si ridurrebbe il consumo elettrico e, di conseguenza, le emissioni di CO_2 derivanti dalla combustione dei combustibili fossili o ancora, la sostituzione delle lampadine incandescenti con altre a basso consumo o a LED, contribuirebbe all'efficienza energetica della casa.

L'immagine mostra la classificazione energetica che può far riferimento sia agli elettrodomestici che agli edifici. Detta classificazione indica il consumo energetico espresso in kWh.

1.3. Eficiência energética

Define-se como a redução do consumo de energia, mantendo os serviços ou padrões de conforto e qualidade de vida. Aplica-se a qualquer aspecto da nossa vida: aos electrodomésticos, à habitação ou ao transporte. Caso se substituíssem os electrodomésticos com mais de 10 anos por outros de classe A, iria reduzir-se o consumo eléctrico e, portanto, as emissões de CO_2 resultantes da queima de combustíveis fósseis. Substituir as lâmpadas incandescentes por outras de baixo consumo ou leds, também contribui para a eficiência energética da casa.

A imagem mostra a classificação energética, seja de um electrodoméstico ou de uma casa. Normalmente, aplica-se ao consumo em kWh de cada elemento.

© Raul J. Garcia   * 1.4

1.4. Sustainable architecture
This concept bears in mind the impact that a building will have during its life cycle: its construction, its use and its ultimate demolishment. It considers issues such as the ease with which materials can be recycled, how much energy and water are needed for its operation and what the impact on the local fauna and flora might be. The increase in world population and the growth of housing space make it necessary to reflect on this topic and apply ground rules and laws to regulate the use of resources and the life cycle of materials.
This house adapts itself to the slope of the ground thereby minimally affecting the natural surroundings. Solar panels are one of its energy-saving systems.

1.4. Nachhaltige Architektur
Bei diesem Konzept wird die Auswirkung eines Gebäudes während seiner gesamten Lebensdauer, d. h., während des Baus, seiner Nutzung und dem abschließenden Abbruch berücksichtigt. Sie hinterfragt, ob die Baumaterialien leicht wiederverwendet werden können, wie viel Energie und Wasser für die Nutzung erforderlich sind oder wie seine Auswirkung auf Fauna und Flora in der Umgebung aussieht. Der Anstieg der Weltbevölkerung und die Vergrößerung des Gebäudeparks zwingen zu einer eingehenden Betrachtung dieses Themas und zur Einsetzung von Vorschriften und Gesetzen, welche den Einsatz der Ressourcen und den Lebenskreislauf der Materialien regeln.
Dieses Haus passt sich der Geländeneigung an, um das natürliche Umfeld so wenig wie möglich zu beeinflussen. Die Solarthermieplatten stellen eines der Energieeinsparungssysteme dar.

1.4. Architecture respectueuse de l'environnement
Ce concept tient compte de l'impact d'une construction durant tout son cycle de vie : pendant sa construction, son utilisation, puis, finalement, sa destruction. Il englobe des questions comme le recyclage des matériaux, les quantités d'énergie et d'eau nécessaires à son fonctionnement ainsi que l'impact d'un bâtiment sur la faune et la flore locales. L'augmentation de la population mondiale conjointement à celle du parc de logements oblige à se pencher sur ces problèmes et à imaginer des normes et des lois pour réguler l'emploi des ressources et le cycle de vie des matériaux.
Cette maison s'adapte au dénivelé du terrain pour réduire au minimum son impact sur son environnement immédiat. Les panneaux solaires thermiques sont l'une des installations permettant d'économiser l'énergie.

1.4. Duurzame architectuur
Dit begrip houdt rekening met het effect dat het gebouw gedurende zijn gehele levenscyclus zal hebben: tijdens de bouw, het gebruik en tenslotte bij de uiteindelijke sloop. Het brengt kwesties ter sprake zoals de mate waarin materialen al dan niet gemakkelijk kunnen worden hergebruikt, hoeveel energie en water er nodig is voor het functioneren ervan of wat het effect op de flora en fauna van de omgeving zal zijn. De groei van de wereldbevolking en de toename van het aantal huizen verplichten ertoe om over dit onderwerp na te denken en om normen en wetten op te stellen die het gebruik van de hulpbronnen en de levenscyclus van de materialen regelen.
Dit huis past zich aan het hoogteverschil van het terrein aan om zo min mogelijk impact op de natuurlijke omgeving te hebben. Een van de gebruikte energiebesparingssystemen zijn de thermische zonnepanelen.

1.4. Arquitectura sostenible
Este concepto tiene en cuenta el impacto que tendrá esta construcción durante todo su ciclo de vida: durante la construcción, su uso y hasta el derribo final. Plantea cuestiones como si podrán los materiales ser fácilmente reciclables, cuánta energía y agua se necesitarán para su funcionamiento o cuál será el impacto en la fauna y la flora del entorno. El crecimiento de la población mundial y el aumento del parque de viviendas obligan a una reflexión sobre este tema y a la puesta en marcha de normativas y leyes que regulen el uso de recursos y el ciclo de vida de los materiales.
Esta casa se adapta al desnivel del terreno para afectar mínimamente al entorno natural. Las placas solares térmicas son uno de los sistemas de ahorro energético.

1.4. Architettura sostenibile
Si tratta di una disciplina che tiene conto dell'impatto che ha ogni costruzione durante il suo intero ciclo di vita, ovvero la costruzione, l'uso e l'abbattimento finale. Prospetta questioni quali la facilità di riciclaggio dei materiali, la quantità d'energia e d'acqua necessarie per il suo funzionamento o il suo impatto sulla fauna e la flora dell'ambiente circostante. La crescita della popolazione mondiale e l'aumento del parco abitazioni comportano una riflessione obbligata su questo concetto e sul varo di normative e leggi che disciplinino l'uso delle risorse e il ciclo di vita dei materiali.
Questa casa si adatta al dislivello del terreno per minimizzare l'impatto sull'ambiente circostante. Le placche solari termiche rappresentano uno dei sistemi di risparmio energetico a nostra disposizione.

1.4. Arquitectura sustentável

Este conceito tem em conta o impacto que esta construção terá durante todo o seu ciclo de vida: durante a construção, no seu uso e acabando na demolição final. Coloca questões, tais como, se os materiais poderão ser facilmente reciclados, quanta energia e água serão necessárias para o seu funcionamento ou qual será o impacto na fauna e na flora do espaço envolvente. O crescimento da população mundial e o aumento do número de habitações obrigam a uma reflexão sobre este tema e à criação de normas e leis que regulem o uso de recursos e o ciclo de vida dos materiais.

Esta casa adapta-se ao desnível do terreno para afectar minimamente o ambiente natural. Os painéis solares térmicos são um dos sistemas de poupança energética.

2. MATERIALS

One of the most important aspects of ecological architecture is the use of low environmental impact construction materials. The main advantages of this are lower CO_2 emissions and a logical use of natural resources.

2. BAUMATERIAL

Auswahl und Einsatz von Baumaterial mit geringer Umweltauswirkung stellen einen der wichtigsten Aspekte der ökologischen Architektur dar. Deren Hauptvorteile sind niedrigere CO_2-Abgaben und ein rationeller Einsatz der Naturressourcen.

2. MATÉRIAUX

Une des options les plus significatives de l'architecture écologique est le choix et l'emploi de matériaux de construction ayant un faible impact sur l'environnement. Ses principaux bienfaits sont la baisse des émissions de CO_2 et l'emploi rationnel des ressources naturelles.

2. MATERIALEN

Een van de belangrijkste aspecten van de ecologische architectuur is de keuze en het gebruik van bouwmaterialen die een laag impact op het milieu hebben. De voornaamste voordelen zijn minder CO_2-uitstoot en een redelijk gebruik van de natuurlijke hulpbronnen.

2. MATERIALES

Uno de los aspectos más importantes de la arquitectura ecológica es la elección y el uso de materiales de construcción de bajo impacto ambiental. Los beneficios principales son menos emisiones de CO_2 y un uso racional de los recursos naturales.

2. MATERIALI

Uno degli aspetti più importanti dell'architettura ecologica è la scelta e l'uso di materiali da costruzione a basso impatto ambientale. I benefici principali sono rappresentati da un più basso livello di emissioni di CO_2 ed un uso razionale delle risorse naturali.

2. MATERIAIS

Um dos aspectos mais importantes da arquitectura ecológica é a escolha e o uso de materiais de construção de baixo impacto ambiental. Os benefícios principais são menos emissões de CO_2 e um uso racional dos recursos naturais.

2.1. Natural materials

Natural construction materials are those requiring little manufacturing processing for their creation. Every process, such as varnishing wood or making a metal beam, has an environmental cost. The best known materials are wood, bamboo or straw, stone, etc. Varnishes can be avoided and environment-friendly lacquers can be substituted; straw can be used as insulation instead of synthetic foams; natural, local stone can be used, etc.

Bamboo is a strong, clean, hard, smooth wood which grows almost everywhere. Its rapid growth makes it a renewable resource.

2.1. Natürliches Baumaterial

Baumaterial mit wenigen Bearbeitungsvorgängen bei der Herstellung wird als natürliches Baumaterial eingestuft. Alle Bearbeitungen wie z. B. Holzlackierung oder die Herstellung eines Metallträgers verursachen Umweltkosten. Zu den bekanntesten natürlichen Baumaterialien gehören Holz, Bambus, Stroh, Stein usw.

* 2.1

Dabei ist es möglich, den Einsatz von Lacken zu vermeiden oder umweltfreundliche Lacke, Stroh statt Kunststoffschaum als Isoliermittel und vor Ort vorhandene Natursteine usw. zu verwenden.
Bambus ist ein widerstandsfähiges, sauberes, hartes und glattes Holz, das fast überall vorhanden ist. Sein schnelles Wachstum macht es zu einer erneuerbaren Ressource.

2.1. Matériaux naturels
Sont dits matériaux naturels, tous les matériaux dont la fabrication n'exige qu'un minimum de transformation, les plus connus étant le bois, le bambou ou la paille et la pierre. Chaque processus, vernir un bois ou usiner une poutre métallique, a un coût environnemental. Il est possible d'éviter les vernis ou de préférer des laques respectueuses du milieu ambiant, de donner la priorité à la paille sur d'autres isolants comme les mousses d'origine synthétique et de favoriser l'usage de matériaux locaux, bois ou pierres.
Le bambou est résistant, propre, dur et lisse, présent pratiquement dans le monde entier. Sa croissance rapide en fait une ressource renouvelable.

2.1. Natuurlijke materialen
Onder natuurlijk bouwmateriaal worden die materialen verstaan die weinig bewerkingsprocessen voor de fabricage vergen. Elk proces, zoals het lakken van hout of de vervaardiging van een metalen balk, heeft zijn milieukosten. Onder de bekendste natuurlijke materialen vallen o.a. hout, bamboe, stro en steen. Zo kan onder meer het gebruik van vernis worden vermeden of kunnen er milieuvriendelijke lakken worden toegepast. Tevens kan de voorkeur gegeven worden aan het gebruik van stro als isolatiemateriaal in plaats van synthetisch schuim of kan natuursteen van plaatselijke herkomst worden gebruikt.
Bamboe is een sterk, schoon, hard en glad hout dat bijna overal ter wereld aanwezig is. De snelle groei maakt het een hernieuwbare hulpbron.

2.1. Materiales naturales
Se consideran materiales de construcción naturales a aquellos que requieren pocos procesos de manufactura para su fabricación. Cada proceso, como el barnizado de una madera o la fabricación de una viga metálica, tiene un coste ambiental. Entre los más conocidos están la madera, el bambú o la paja, la piedra, etc. Se puede evitar el uso de barnices o usar lacados respetuosos con el medio ambiente, priorizar el uso de la paja como aislante en lugar de espumas sintéticas, usar piedra natural de origen local, etc.
El bambú es una madera resistente, limpia, dura y lisa, presente en casi todo el mundo. Su rápido crecimiento lo convierte en un recurso renovable.

2.1. Materiali naturali
Rientrano tra i materiali di costruzione considerati naturali quelli per la cui fabbricazione è necessario un breve processo di manifattura. Ogni processo, quale la verniciatura del legno o la fabbricazione di una trave metallica ha un costo ambientale. Tra i materiali naturali più noti ricordiamo il legno, il bambù, la paglia, la pietra, ecc. È possibile evitare l'uso di vernici o usare lacche rispettose dell'ambiente, dare priorità all'uso della paglia come isolante anziché a quello di schiume sintetiche, usare la pietra naturale d'origine locale, ecc.
Il bambù è un legno resistente, pulito, duro e liscio, presente in quasi tutto il mondo. La sua rapida crescita fa di questo legno una risorsa rinnovabile.

2.1. Materiais naturais
Considera-se material de construção natural aquele que requer poucos processos de manufacturação para o seu fabrico. Cada processo, tal como o envernizamento de uma madeira ou o fabrico de uma viga metálica, tem um custo ambiental. Entre os mais conhecidos estão a madeira, o bambu ou a palha, a pedra, etc. Pode evitar-se o uso de vernizes ou usar lacas que respeitem o ambiente, dar prioridade ao uso da palha como isolante em vez de espumas sintéticas, usar pedra natural de origem local, etc.
O bambu é uma madeira resistente, limpa, dura e lisa, presente em quase todo o mundo. O seu rápido crescimento converte-o num recurso renovável.

2.2. Local materials
Local materials carry a lower cost as being from the area they are cheaper. They also have a lower environmental cost as CO_2 emissions generated by their transport are reduced. Tropical wood is a beautiful and strong material but the environmental cost of transporting it makes its use unadvisable in the USA. Some uses of local construction materials are adobe or tapial (rammed earth), techniques using clay; a primary and local material. The area's wood and stone should also be kept in mind.
This Bangladesh school, the work of Anna Heringer and Eike Roswag, is made of adobe and bamboo, common local materials.

* 2.2

2.2. Lokales Baumaterial

Baumaterial lokaler Herkunft ist günstiger, da es in der Gegend häufig vorhanden ist. Seine Umweltkosten sind aufgrund der geringeren CO_2-Abgaben beim Transport niedriger. Tropenhölzer sind zwar schöne und widerstandsfähige Baumaterialien, deren Umweltkosten beim Transport jedoch von ihrem Einsatz in Europa abraten. Als Beispiele für den Bau mit lokalen Baumaterialien gelten Lehmziegel oder Lehmwände, bei denen das lokale und primäre Baumaterial Lehm eingesetzt wird. Auch Hölzer oder Steine aus der Region fallen unter diese Kategorie.

Diese Schule in Bangladesh, ein Bau von Anna Heringer und Eike Roswag, wurde aus Lehmziegeln und Bambus, die in großer Fülle in dieser Region vorhanden sind, erbaut.

2.2. Matériaux locaux

Les matériaux d'origine locale reviennent moins chers, puisqu'ils sont abondants, et ont un coût environnemental moindre puisqu'ils sont sur place. Les émissions de CO_2 dues au transport sont réduites. Les arbres tropicaux sont des bois nobles et résistants, mais le coût environnemental de leur acheminement devrait inciter à s'abstenir de les importer pour les utiliser en Europe. Quelques exemples de construction en matériaux locaux sont l'adobe ou le pisé, techniques à base de terre, matériau primaire universellement disponible. Les bois ou pierres locales ne sont pas à négliger.

Cette école au Bangladesh, œuvre de Anna Heringer et Eike Roswag, est en adobe et bambou, matériaux abondants dans ce pays.

2.2. Plaatselijke materialen

Materialen van plaatselijke oorsprong hebben lagere kosten. Het feit dat ze gewoon in de streek voorkomen betekent namelijk dat ze goedkoper zijn en minder milieukosten opleveren, want de CO_2-uitstoot tengevolge van het transport is eveneens minder. Tropisch hout is een mooi en sterk materiaal, maar door de milieukosten van het transport wordt het gebruik in Europa afgeraden. Enkele voorbeelden van de bouw met plaatselijke materialen zijn adobe of stampleem, technieken waarbij grond, een primair plaatselijk materiaal, wordt gebruikt. Ook lokaal hout of steen moeten in acht worden genomen.

Deze school in Bangladesh, het werk van Anna Heringer en Eike Roswag, is gemaakt van adobe en bamboe, materialen die veel in de streek voorkomen.

2.2. Materiales locales

Los materiales de origen local tienen un coste reducido, pues al ser comunes en la zona son más baratos, y un menor coste ambiental, pues las emisiones de CO_2 derivadas del transporte también son menores. Una madera tropical es un material bello y resistente, pero los costes ambientales del transporte desaconsejan su uso en Europa. Algunos ejemplos de construcción con materiales locales son el adobe o el tapial, técnicas que utilizan tierra, un material primario y local. Las maderas o piedras de la zona también deben tenerse en cuenta.

Esta escuela en Bangladesh, obra de Anna Heringer y Eike Roswag, se ha fabricado con adobe y bambú, materiales abundantes en la zona.

2.2. Materiali locali

I materiali d'origine locale hanno un costo inferiore poiché, essendo comuni nella zona, sono più economici ed hanno un minore costo ambientale, le emissioni di CO_2 derivanti dal trasporto, infatti, sono inferiori. I legni tropicali sono materiali belli e resistenti, ma i costi ambientali del trasporto ne sconsigliano l'uso in Europa. Alcuni esempi di costruzione con materiali locali sono quelle in adobe o tapial che ricorrono a tecniche che utilizzano la terra per produrre un materiale primario e locale. È bene tenere conto anche del legno e della pietra locale.

Questa scuola del Bangladesh, opera di Anna Heringer e Eike Roswag, è stata fabbricata con adobe e bambù, materiali abbondanti nella zona.

2.2. Materiais locais

Os materiais de origem local têm um custo menor, visto que ao serem comuns na zona são mais baratos, e têm um menor custo ambiental, uma vez que as emissões de CO_2 derivadas do transporte também são menores. Uma madeira tropical é um material belo e resistente, mas os custos ambientais do transporte desaconselham o seu uso na Europa. Alguns exemplos de construção com materiais locais são o adobe ou a taipa, técnicas que utilizam terra, um material primário e local. As madeiras ou pedras da zona também devem ser tidas em conta.

Esta escola no Bangladeche, obra de Anna Heringer e Eike Roswag, foi construída com adobe e bambu, materiais abundantes na zona.

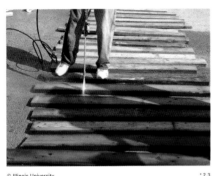

© Illinois University   * 2.3

2.3. Recyclable, recycled and salvaged materials

Recyclable materials, such as glass, can be easily reused. Recycled materials come from those which can have a second use, like plywood; some can be recycled again once the house's life cycle has come to an end. Salvaged materials are boards, beams or materials from other constructions. Re-use saves on transport and prevents resources being uncontrollably used. There should be no waste either during their creation or when they are no longer useable.
Strips of wood from an old silo were washed and treated with linseed oil to become part of the outdoor flooring.

2.3. Wiederverwertbare, wiederverwertete und wiedergewonnene Baumaterialien

Wiederverwertbares Baumaterial wie Glas kann leicht wiederverwendet werden. Wiederverwertete Baumaterialien aus Abfällen werden für einen weiteren Zweck, wie z. B. Holzfurnier, verwendet. Einige darunter können nach der Lebensdauer des Hauses wieder verwendet werden. Wiedergewonnenes Baumaterial sind Bretter, Träger oder andere Baumaterialien aus anderen Bauten. Die Wiederverwendung spart Transportkosten und verursacht keinen unkontrollierten Ressourcenverbrauch. Bei ihrer Herstellung wie auch am Ende ihrer Lebensdauer dürfen keine Abfälle entstehen.
Die Leisten eines ehemaligen Silos wurden gewaschen und mit Leinöl behandelt, um als Außendielen eingesetzt werden zu können.

2.3. Matériaux recyclables, recyclés et réutilisés

Les matériaux recyclables, comme le verre, peuvent facilement être réemployés. D'autres matériaux recyclés sont fabriqués à partir de déchets transformés, comme le bois contreplaqué ; certains peuvent être à nouveau recyclés une fois le cycle de vie de la maison achevé. Les matériaux réutilisés sont les planches, poutres et autres madriers provenant d'anciennes constructions. La réutilisation des matériaux permet des économies sur le transport et évite un gaspillage inconsidéré des ressources. Leur fabrication et leur élimination ne doivent pas produire de déchets.
Les liteaux d'un ancien silo ont été nettoyés et traités à l'huile de lin pour être utilisés dans le parquet extérieur.

2.3. Recyclebare, gerecyclede en herwonnen materialen

Recyclebare materialen zoals glas kunnen gemakkelijk worden hergebruikt. Gerecyclede materialen worden gemaakt van afval en worden voor een tweede toepassing verwerkt, zoals multiplex. Sommige materialen kunnen na de levenscyclus opnieuw worden gebruikt. Herwonnen materialen zijn planken, balken of andere materialen van andere constructies. Het opnieuw benutten daarvan bespaart transport en verspilt hulpbronnen niet op ongecontroleerde wijze. De materialen mogen geen afval produceren, noch tijdens de fabricage noch na afloop van hun levensduur.
De latjes van een oude silo zijn gewassen en met lijnzaadolie behandeld zodat ze gebruikt konden worden voor de buitenvloer.

2.3. Materiales reciclables, reciclados y recuperados

Los materiales reciclables pueden ser reutilizados fácilmente, como el cristal. Los reciclados se realizan a partir de residuos con un segundo uso, como la madera contrachapada; algunos pueden volver a reciclarse una vez finalizado el ciclo de vida de la casa. Los materiales recuperados son tablones, vigas u otros materiales de otras construcciones. El aprovechamiento de materiales ahorra transporte y no gasta recursos incontroladamente. No deben generarse residuos durante su fabricación ni al finalizar su vida útil.
Los listones de un antiguo silo se lavaron y trataron con aceite de linaza para que formaran parte de la tarima exterior.

2.3. Materiali riciclabili, riciclati e recuperati

I materiali riciclabili possono essere riutilizzati facilmente, ad esempio il vetro. I materiali riciclati sono realizzati a partire da residui con un secondo uso, come il compensato; alcuni si essi possono essere nuovamente riciclati al termine del ciclo di vita dell'edificio. I materiali recuperati sono rappresentati da tavoloni, travi o da materiali di altre costruzioni. Il riutilizzo consente di risparmiare trasporto e di evitare il consuma di risorse in modo incontrollato. Non devono generarsi residui né durante la loro fabbricazione né al termine della loro vita utile.
I listelli di un vecchio silo sono lavorati e trattati con olio di semi di lino per formare parte della predella esterna.

2.3. Materiais recicláveis, reciclados e recuperados

Os materiais recicláveis podem ser facilmente reutilizados, como, por exemplo, o vidro. Os reciclados são produzidos a partir de resíduos com um segundo uso, como a madeira contraplacada; alguns podem voltar a ser reciclados uma vez terminado o ciclo de vida da casa. Os materiais recuperados são tábuas, vigas ou outros materiais de outras construções. O reaproveitamento permite poupar no transporte e não gasta recursos descontroladamente. Não devem ser gerados resíduos nem durante o seu fabrico nem quando termina a sua vida útil.

As ripas de um antigo silo foram lavadas e tratadas com óleo de linhaça para fazerem parte do estrado exterior.

*2.4

2.4. FSC, low VOC, low-e...
When talking about wood with certified origins the initials FSC (Forest Stewardship Council) and PEFC (Pan European Forest Council) are used. These are two associations ensuring the controlled origin of wood and guarantee that unprotected forests are not exploited. Low VOC refers to varnishes and paints with low organic, volatile components, elements which become gasses or vapours. The Low-e concept refers to glass with low thermal emission, reducing thermal loss while allowing light to enter.

Certified wood comes from land which does not reduce forest area. Woods are vital to control erosion and regulate precipitation.

2.4. FSC, Low VOC, Low-e...
Wenn es um Hölzer mit zertifizierter Herkunft geht, spricht man von Abkürzungen wie FSC (Forest Stewardship Council) und PEFC (Pan European Forest Council). Diese beiden Verbände garantieren die kontrollierte Herkunft und gewährleisten, dass keine ungeschützten Waldflächen abgebaut werden. Als low VOC werden Lacke und Farben mit niedrigem Anteil an flüchtigen organischen Bestandteilen, die sich in Gase oder Dampf verwandeln, bezeichnet. Das Low-e-Konzept bezieht sich auf Scheiben mit niedriger Wärmeabgabe, welche die übertragene Wärmeaufnahme senken und sichtbares Licht durchlassen.

Zertifiziertes Holz kommt aus Bebauungen, welche den Forstbestand nicht reduzieren. Die Wälder sind unbedingt zur Kontrolle der Erosion und Niederschlagsregulierung erforderlich.

2.4. FSC, étiquette COV, basse-émissivité...
Quand on parle de bois issu de forêts éco-certifiées, on utilise les sigles FSC (Forest Stewardship Council) et PEFC (Pan European Forest Council). Ce sont deux des labels qui garantissent que le bois provient de forêts gérées et non de la destruction de massifs non protégés. L'étiquette COV apposée sur les vernis et peintures informe du taux de rejet de composés organiques volatils, substances chimiques qui se libèrent dans l'atmosphère sous forme de gaz ou de vapeur. Le concept de *basse émissivité* désigne des verres à faible émission thermique, qui réduisent les échanges thermiques en laissant passer la lumière du jour.

Les bois bénéficiant de labels viennent de forêts gérées, ce qui signifie que les arbres coupés sont replantés. Leur utilisation ne réduit pas la masse forestière. Les forêts sont indispensables pour contrôler l'érosion et réguler les précipitations.

2.4. FSC, Low VOC, Low-e...
Wanneer gesproken wordt over gecertificeerd hout worden de afkortingen FSC (Forest Stewardship Council) en PEFC (Pan European Forest Council) gebruikt. Dit zijn twee van de organisaties die garant staan voor de gecontroleerde herkomst en waarborgen dat geen onbeschermde bosoppervlakken worden geëxploiteerd. De *low VOC* heeft betrekking op vernissen en verven met een laag gehalte aan vluchtige organische stoffen die in gassen of dampen veranderen. Het *Low-e* begrip verwijst naar glas met een lage warmte-emissie waardoor de overgebrachte warmtewinst verminderd en zichtbaar licht doorgelaten wordt.

Gecertificeerd hout komt van bosbedrijven die de bosmassa niet verminderen. Bossen zijn onontbeerlijk om de erosie te controleren en de neerslag te regelen.

2.4. FSC, bajo COV, Low-e...
Cuando se habla de maderas de origen certificado se utilizan las siglas FSC (Forest Stewardship Council) y el PEFC (Pan European Forest Council), dos de las asociaciones que aseguran el origen controlado y garantizan que no se explotan superficies forestales desprotegidas. Los barnices y pinturas con bajo COV son aquellos con un bajo porcentaje componentes orgánicos volátiles, elementos que se convierten en gases o vapores. El concepto Low-e se refiere a cristales de baja emisión térmica, que reducen la ganancia térmica transmitida y dejan pasar la luz visible.

La madera certificada procede de explotaciones que no reducen la masa forestal. Los bosques son imprescindibles para controlar la erosión y regular las precipitaciones.

2.4. FSC, Low VOC, Low-e...

Quando si parla di legno con certificato d'origine si utilizzano le sigle FSC (Forest Stewardship Council) e PEFC (Pan European Forest Council) che sono due delle associazioni che ne controllano l'origine garantendo che non siano ottenuti dallo sfruttamento di superfici forestali non protette. Il *low VOC* definisce le vernici e le pitture a bassa percentuale di solventi organici volatili, elementi che si convertono in gas e vapori. Il concetto *Low-e* fa riferimento a vetri a bassa emissione termica che riducono il guadagno di calore trasmesso e lasciano filtrare la luce visibile.

* Il legno certificato proviene da sfruttamenti che non riducono la massa forestale. I boschi sono imprescindibili per controllare l'erosione e regolare le precipitazioni.

2.4. FSC, Low VOC, Low-e...

Quando se fala de madeiras de origem certificada utilizam-se as siglas FSC (Forest Stewardship Council) e PEFC (Pan European Forest Council), duas das associações que asseguram a origem controlada e garantem que não se exploram superfícies florestais desprotegidas. *Low VOC* define os vernizes e tintas com uma baixa percentagem de compostos orgânicos voláteis, elementos que se convertem em gases ou vapores. O conceito *Low-e* refere-se a vidros de baixa emissão térmica, que reduzem a carga térmica transmitida e deixam passar a luz visível.

* A madeira certificada procede de explorações que não reduzem a massa florestal. As florestas são imprescindíveis para controlar a erosão e regular a precipitação.

3. PREFABRICATED BUILDINGS

Prefabricated construction is a group of industrialised constructive systems applicable to housing, hospitals, industries, etc. It reduces costs and construction time. The environmental advantages are lower CO_2 emissions resulting from the manufacturing and transport of materials.

3. FERTIGBAU

Unter Fertigbau versteht man industrialisierte Bauweisen für Wohnhäuser, Krankenhäuser, Industrien usw. Sie bieten die Möglichkeit, Kosten und Bauzeit zu senken. Der Vorteil für die Umwelt besteht in der Senkung der CO_2-Abgaben, die sich aus der Herstellung und dem Transport der Baumaterialien ableiten.

3. CONSTRUIRE EN PRÉFABRIQUÉ

La construction en préfabriqué recourt à un ensemble de techniques faisant appel à des produits industriels qui peuvent être utilisés pour bâtir des logements, des hôpitaux, des industries, etc. Leur emploi permet de réduire les coûts et la durée des chantiers. Leur avantage pour le milieu ambiant est la réduction des émissions de CO_2 liées à la fabrication et au transport des matériaux.

3. PREFAB BOUW

Prefab bouw is een reeks geïndustrialiseerde bouwsystemen toegepast op onder andere woningen, ziekenhuizen en fabrieken. Het is een manier om kosten te verlagen en de bouwtijd te reduceren. Het voordeel voor het milieu is de reductie van de bij de fabricage en het transport van de materialen uitgestoten CO_2.

3. CONSTRUCCIÓN PREFABRICADA

La construcción prefabricada es un conjunto de sistemas constructivos industrializados aplicados a viviendas, hospitales, industrias, etc. Es una manera de reducir costes y también el tiempo de construcción. La ventaja para el medio ambiente es la reducción de las emisiones de CO_2 derivadas de la fabricación y el transporte de los materiales.

3. COSTRUZIONE PREFABBRICATA

La costruzione prefabbricata rappresenta un insieme di sistemi costruttivi industrializzati applicati alle abitazioni, agli ospedali, alle industrie, ecc. Si tratta di una maniera di ridurre costi e abbattere i tempi di costruzione. Il vantaggio per l'ambiente è la riduzione delle emissioni di CO_2 derivanti dalla fabbricazione e dal trasporto dei materiali.

3. CONSTRUÇÃO PRÉ-FABRICADA

A construção pré-fabricada é um conjunto de sistemas construtivos industrializados aplicados a habitações, hospitais, indústrias, etc. É uma forma de reduzir os custos e o tempo de construção. A vantagem para o ambiente é a redução das emissões de CO_2 derivadas do fabrico e do transporte dos materiais.

© Adrian Gregorutti

*3.1

3.1. Prefabricated elements

Panels and other standard sized elements are made in the factory and transported for on site assembling. In these cases it is only necessary to build or assemble the foundations on which the pieces will be put together. Various pieces are available: structural insulated panels (SIP), concrete elements, etc. In addition to speed, prefabricated constructions imply a saving on resources, as careful design avoids superfluous materials which entail higher costs.
The façade is made up of waterproof, fibrocement panels, cut in the factory and assembled on site. The accuracy of the measurements avoided added expenses.

3.1. Fertigbauteile

Paneele und weitere Teile mit Standardabmessungen werden im Werk hergestellt und zum Einbau vor Ort transportiert. In diesen Fällen muss nur das Fundament, auf dem die Teile aufgebaut werden, erbaut oder aufgestellt werden. Die verschiedenen Teile wie Isolierpaneele (SIP), Betonteile usw. sind sehr zahlreich. Neben der Schnelligkeit stellen die Fertigmaterialien eine Ressourceneinsparung dar, da ein sorgfältiger Entwurf Materialüberschuss mit evtl. Mehrkosten verhindert.
Die Fassade besteht aus wasserdichten Faserzementpaneelen, die im Werk geschnitten und vor Ort montiert wurden. Die Präzision ihrer Abmessungen vermied übermäßige Kosten.

3.1. Éléments préfabriqués

Les panneaux et autres éléments de dimensions standard sont construits en usine et acheminés pour être assemblés sur site. Il suffit donc de prévoir les fondations sur lesquelles seront montés les différents éléments. Il en existe une multitude : panneaux isolants (SIP), pièces en béton, etc. Outre la rapidité d'assemblage, le recours aux éléments préfabriqués entraîne une économie des ressources, car le soin apporté au plan évite des excédents de matériaux qui feraient monter le coût.
La façade est en panneaux de fibrociment imperméable, manufacturés en usine et assemblés in situ. La précision des dimensions évite les dépenses superflues.

3.1. Prefab elementen

Panelen en andere materialen met standaardmaten worden in de fabriek geproduceerd en voor de montage ter plaatse vervoerd. In deze gevallen hoeft alleen een fundering te worden aangelegd waarop de verschillende onderdelen in elkaar zullen worden gezet. Er zijn talrijke materialen zoals o.a. SIP-panelen, betondelen. Naast de snelle montage worden met prefab elementen eveneens hulpbronnen bespaard, want een zorgvuldig ontwerp voorkomt overtollig materiaal dat hogere kosten met zich mee brengt.
De gevel bestaat uit waterdichte vezelcementpanelen, die in de fabriek uitgesneden en ter plaatse geassembleerd zijn. Nauwkeurige maten vermijden buitensporige kosten.

3.1. Elementos prefabricados

Los paneles y otras piezas de medidas estándar se construyen en la fábrica y se transportan para su montaje in situ. Así, sólo es necesario construir o montar unos cimientos sobre los que ensamblar las piezas. Existen numerosos tipos: paneles aislantes (SIP), piezas de hormigón, etc. Además de rapidez, los prefabricados suponen un ahorro de recursos, pues un diseño cuidadoso evitará excedentes de material que supondrían un mayor coste.
La fachada está compuesta de paneles de fibrocemento impermeable, tallados en fábrica y ensamblados in situ. La precisión de las medidas evitó un gasto excesivo.

3.1. Elementi prefabbricati

I pannelli ed altri pezzi dalle misure standard si costruiscono in fabbrica e si trasportano per il loro montaggio in situ. In questi casi è necessario soltanto costruire o montare delle fondamenta sulle quali dovranno essere poi assemblati i pezzi. Esistono innumerevoli pezzi: pannelli isolanti (SIP), pezzi in calcestruzzo, ecc. Oltre alla velocità, i prefabbricati presuppongono un risparmio di risorse giacché un progetto accurato eviterà eccedenze di materiale che supporrebbero un aumento dei costi.
La facciata è composta da pannelli in fibrocemento impermeabile, tagliati in fabbrica e assemblati in situ. La precisione delle misure evitò una spesa eccessiva.

3.1. Elementos pré-fabricados

Os painéis e outras peças de medidas standard constroem-se na fábrica e transportam-se para a sua montagem in situ. Nestes casos apenas é necessário construir ou montar alguns alicerces sobre os quais serão montadas as peças. Existem inúmeras peças: painéis isolantes (SIP), peças de betão, etc. Além de rapidez, os pré-fabricados implicam uma poupança de recursos, visto que uma concepção cuidadosa evitará excedentes de material que implicariam um custo superior.
A fachada é constituída por painéis de fibrocimento impermeável, produzidos na fábrica e montados in situ. A precisão das medidas evitou um gasto excessivo.

3.2. Modular houses

Modular construction involves factory-made modules, either in their entirety or a set percentage. Once the module has been delivered, the installations and other elements such as doors and windows are assembled. Prefabricated modules are gaining popularity in residential architecture as the advantages are greatest when they are made in batches, thus further reducing costs. Prefabricated construction is not inferior in quality nor does it last less.

Building no longer takes months; with prefabricated elements it takes just weeks or even days, depending on the type of structure.

3.2. Modulhäuser

Beim Modulbau wird das Modul vollständig oder in einem bestimmten Prozentsatz im Werk hergestellt. Nach dem Transport werden Installationen und weitere Elemente wie Türen und Fenster in das Modul eingebaut. Fertigmodule sind immer stärker in der Wohnhausarchitektur vertreten. Ihre Vorteile erhöhen sich, wenn sie serienmäßig gefertigt werden, da die Kosten dadurch weiter sinken. Der Fertigbau stellt keine Bauweise mit niedrigerer Qualität oder geringerer Lebensdauer dar.

Der Bau mit Fertigbaumaterial kann sich - je nach Gebäudeart - von Monaten auf Wochen oder sogar Tage reduzieren.

3.2. Maisons modulaires

La construction modulaire utilise des modules fabriqués en atelier, soit complètement, soit selon un pourcentage déterminé. Une fois le module en place, on fait les installations et l'on ajoute les huisseries. Les modules préfabriqués permettent des gains de place. Ils sont encore plus avantageux fabriqués en série puisque les coûts diminuent. Les constructions préfabriquées ne sont pas de qualité inférieure et n'ont pas une durée de vie inférieure aux autres.

Selon le type de bâtiment, construire avec des éléments préfabriqués réduit la durée du chantier de quelques mois à quelques semaines, voire quelques jours.

3.2. Modulaire bouwsystemen

Bij modulaire bouw wordt de module volledig of voor een bepaald percentage op de werkplaats gemaakt. Nadat de module is vervoerd, worden de verschillende voorzieningen en andere elementen, zoals deuren en ramen, geïnstalleerd. Prefab modules winnen terrein binnen de woningarchitectuur. De voordelen zijn groter wanneer de modules in serie worden gefabriceerd, aangezien de kosten dan aanzienlijk lager zijn. De prefab bouw is geen bouw van lagere kwaliteit en heeft evenmin een kortere levensduur.

De bouw met prefab elementen kan maanden of weken duren en zelfs dagen, afhankelijk van het soort gebouw.

3.2. Casas modulares

La construcción modular utiliza módulos fabricados en talleres, ya sea completamente o en un porcentaje determinado. Una vez transportado el módulo, se montan las instalaciones y otros elementos, como puertas o ventanas. Los módulos prefabricados están ganando espacio en la arquitectura residencial. Las ventajas son mayores cuando se fabrican en serie, pues se reducen más los costes. La construcción prefabricada no es de menor calidad ni dura menos.

La construcción prefabricada puede reducirse a meses, semanas o incluso días, dependiendo del tipo de edificio.

3.2. Case modulari

Il sistema di costruzione modulare prevede la fabbricazione dei moduli in laboratorio, sia nella loro totalità che in una determinata percentuale. A trasporto eseguito si procede al montaggio delle installazioni e degli altri elementi come, ad esempio, gli infissi. I moduli prefabbricati stanno guadagnando terreno nell'architettura residenziale. I vantaggi sono maggiori quando vengono fabbricati in serie dato che in questo modo si contribuisce all'abbattimento dei costi. La costruzione prefabbricata non è una costruzione di qualità inferiore o di minore durata.

La costruzione con prefabbricati può durare mesi o settimane o addirittura giorni, secondo il tipo di edificio.

3.2. Casas modulares

A construção modular fabrica o módulo em oficinas, seja na totalidade ou numa determinada percentagem. Uma vez transportado o módulo, montam-se as especialidades e outros elementos, como portas ou janelas. Os módulos pré-fabricados estão a ganhar espaço na arquitetura residencial. As vantagens são maiores quando se fabricam em série, pois reduzem-se mais os custos. A construção pré-fabricada não é uma construção de qualidade inferior nem dura menos.

Ao optar-se por pré-fabricados a construção pode passar de meses a semanas ou até dias, dependendo do tipo de edifício.

© Resolution: 4 Architecture   * 3.2

4. PASSIVE SYSTEMS

Passive systems are strategies which aim to improve home energy efficiency without elements which generate artificial energy.

4. PASSIVE SYSTEME

Als passive Systeme werden Strategien bezeichnet, die eine Verbesserung der Energieeffizienz der Wohnhäuser ohne Elemente zur künstlichen Energieerzeugung anstreben.

4. SYSTÈMES PASSIFS

Par systèmes passifs, on désigne toutes les stratégies visant à améliorer l'efficacité énergétique des constructions sans faire appel à des installations produisant de l'énergie.

4. PASSIEVE SYSTEMEN

Passieve systemen zijn strategieën die op zoek zijn naar de verbetering van de energie-efficiëntie van woningen zonder elementen die kunstmatige energie produceren.

4. SISTEMAS PASIVOS

Los sistemas pasivos son aquellas estrategias que buscan mejorar la eficiencia energética de las residencias sin elementos que generen energía artificial.

4. SISTEMI PASSIVI

I sistemi passivi sono rappresentati da quelle strategie che intendono migliorare l'efficienza energetica delle residenze senza elementi che generino energia artificiale.

4. SISTEMAS PASSIVOS

Os sistemas passivos são aquelas estratégias que procuram melhorar a eficiência energética das residências sem elementos que gerem energia artificial.

4.1. Position

A good position is essential for energy efficiency. Mountain houses or beach homes are not the same thing and it is advisable to choose materials well and study the position of the house for the best possible energy use. Thermal mass is based on the ability of materials to absorb heat and release it hours later. Thus, the more exposure to the sun, the less heating is needed. Stone or concrete are materials which absorb heat well.
Glass affords inside lighting and allows heat to enter. Accumulated warmth is released during the night and reduces the need for heating.

4.1. Ausrichtung

Eine gute Ausrichtung ist für die Energieeffizienz grundlegend. Eine Berghütte ist kein Strandhaus, sodass empfohlen wird, das richtige Baumaterial auszuwählen und die Ausrichtung für eine gute Energieleistung zu prüfen. Die Wärmemasse basiert auf der Fähigkeit der Baumaterialien, Wärme aufzunehmen und sie Stunden später wieder abzugeben. Daher ist bei höherer Sonneneinstrahlung weniger Heizung erforderlich. Stein oder Beton sind Baumaterialien, die Wärme gut absorbieren.
Glas ermöglicht die Innenbeleuchtung und den Wärmeeintritt. Die kumulierte Wärme wird nachts abgegeben und senkt den Heizbedarf.

4.1. Orientation

Une bonne orientation est essentielle si l'on vise l'efficacité énergétique. On ne construit pas un refuge de montagne comme une maison sur la plage. Mais dans un cas comme dans l'autre, le choix des matériaux et l'étude de l'orientation sont nécessaires pour maximiser le rendement énergétique. L'inertie thermique indique l'aptitude des matériaux à absorber la chaleur et à la restituer des heures plus tard. Plus l'ensoleillement est prolongé, moins le chauffage est nécessaire. La pierre ou le béton sont des matériaux qui absorbent bien la chaleur.
Le verre permet d'éclairer l'intérieur tout en laissant entrer la chaleur. La chaleur accumulée le jour est restituée pendant la nuit, ce qui réduit le besoin de chauffage.

4.1. Ligging

Een goede ligging is fundamenteel voor energie-efficiëntie. Een berghut is niet hetzelfde als een huis aan het strand. Vandaar dat wordt aanbevolen om voor een goed energierendement de juiste materialen te kiezen

© Charles Lindsay   * 4.1

en de ligging te bestuderen. De thermische massa wordt gebaseerd op het vermogen van de materialen om warmte te absorberen en deze uren later af te scheiden, zodat bij een hogere blootstelling aan de zon minder verwarming nodig is. Steen of beton zijn materialen die goed warmte absorberen.

Glas maakt de verlichting van het interieur en de warmtetoevoer mogelijk. De verzamelde warmte komt 's nachts vrij waardoor minder verwarming noodzakelijk is.

4.1. Orientación

Una buena orientación es primordial para una eficiencia energética. No es lo mismo un refugio de montaña que una casa en la playa, así que se recomienda escoger los materiales y estudiar la orientación para un buen rendimiento energético. La masa térmica se basa en la capacidad de los materiales de absorber calor y desprenderlo horas después, por tanto, cuanto más soleamiento, menos calefacción se necesita. La piedra o el hormigón son materiales que absorben bien el calor.

El cristal permite la iluminación del interior y la entrada de calor. El calor acumulado se desprende durante la noche y reduce la necesidad de calefacción.

4.1. Orientamento

Un buon orientamento è primordiale per l'efficienza energetica. Un rifugio di montagna si differenzia, infatti, da una casa al mare, per questo motivo si raccomanda di scegliere i materiali e di studiare l'orientamento per una buona resa energetica. La massa termica si basa sulla capacità dei materiali di assorbire il calore e di liberarlo alcune ore dopo, quindi ad una maggiore insolazione corrisponde una minore necessità di riscaldamento. La pietra o il calcestruzzo sono materiali che assorbono bene il calore.

Il vetro consente l'illuminazione degli interni e l'entrata del calore. Il calore accumulato viene liberato durante la notte e riduce la necessità di riscaldamento.

4.1. Orientação

Uma boa orientação é primordial para uma eficiência energética. Um refúgio de montanha não é o mesmo que uma casa na praia, pelo que é recomendável escolher os materiais e estudar a orientação para um bom rendimento energético. A massa térmica baseia-se na capacidade dos materiais absorverem calor e libertarem-no horas depois, pelo que quanto mais exposição solar, menos aquecimento artificial. A pedra ou o betão são materiais que absorvem bem o calor.

O vidro permite a iluminação do interior e a entrada de calor. O calor acumulado é libertado durante a noite e reduz a necessidade de aquecimento artificial.

4.2. Cross ventilation

If the area's breezes and the position of windows, doors and balconies have been factored in, air currents can be taken advantage of to cool the house and avoid or reduce the use of air conditioning. A cool tower is another mechanism for cooling as it forces out hot air through openings in the upper part of the house.

The sections show a number of ways to cool the inside. Bioclimatic design helps eliminate hot air from the house.

4.2. Querbelüftung

Bei Berücksichtigung der Luftströmungen im Gebiet und der Fenster-, Tür- und Balkonanordnung, können die Luftströmungen zur Abkühlung des Hauses genutzt werden. Auf diese Art können Klimaanlagen vermieden oder reduziert werden. Der Luftkamin ist ein weiterer Mechanismus zur Abkühlung der Innenräume, da er dank seiner Öffnungen im oberen Hausbereich den Austritt der warmen Luft fördert.

Die Abschnitte zeigen unterschiedliche Arten zur Kühlung des Innenraums. Das bioklimatische Design erleichtert die Abführung der Warmluft aus dem Haus.

4.2. Ventilation croisée

Si l'on a étudié la circulation de l'air autour de la construction et l'emplacement des fenêtres, des portes et des balcons, on peut profiter des vents pour rafraîchir la maison et se dispenser de climatisation ou réduire son utilisation. L'extracteur d'air est une autre solution pour réduire la température d'un intérieur puisqu'il permet l'évacuation de l'air chaud par des ouvertures pratiquées dans la partie supérieure de la maison.

Les croquis en coupes montrent plusieurs manières de refroidir un intérieur. La conception bioclimatique favorise l'évacuation de l'air chaud à l'extérieur de la maison.

4.2. Kruisventilatie

Als rekening is gehouden met de luchtstromen van de streek en de plaats van ramen, deuren en balkons, kunnen de stromingen worden benut om het huis te koelen en het gebruik van airco's op te heffen of te

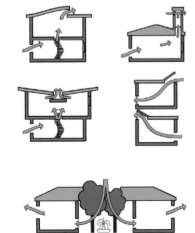

*4.2

reduceren. Een luchtkoker is een ander mechanisme dat het interieur koelt. Het bevordert namelijk de afvoer van warme lucht dankzij openingen aan de bovenkant van het huis.

De doorsneden tonen verschillende manieren om het interieur te verfrissen. Het bioklimatische ontwerp vereenvoudigt de afvoer van warme lucht uit huis.

4.2. Ventilación cruzada

Si se han tenido en cuenta las corrientes de aire de la zona y la ubicación de las ventanas, puertas y balcones, se podrán aprovechar las corrientes para refrigerar la casa y eliminar o reducir la utilización del aire acondicionado. La chimenea de aire es otro de los mecanismos útiles para refrigerar los interiores de las viviendas, pues potencia la salida del aire caliente gracias a aberturas en la parte superior de la casa.

Los esquemas de las secciones muestran diferentes formas de refrescar el interior. El diseño bioclimático facilita la evacuación de aire caliente fuera de la casa.

4.2. Ventilazione incrociata

Se si è tenuto conto delle correnti d'aria della zona e dell'ubicazione delle finestre, delle porte e dei balconi, si potranno sfruttare le correnti per refrigerare la casa ed eliminare o ridurre l'aria condizionata. Il camino ad aria forzata è un altro dei meccanismi che refrigerano gli interni in quanto potenzia la fuoriuscita dell'aria calda grazie alle aperture nella parte superiore della casa.

Le sezioni mostrano diverse maniere di refrigerare gli interni. Il progetto bioclimatico facilita l'evacuazione dell'aria calda dall'edificio.

4.2. Ventilação cruzada

Caso se tenha tido em conta as correntes de ar da zona e a localização das janelas, portas e varandas, poderão aproveitar-se as correntes para refrescar a casa e eliminar ou reduzir o uso de ar condicionado. A chaminé de ar é outro dos mecanismos que refrescam os interiores, pois potencia a saída do ar quente graças a aberturas na zona superior da casa.

As secções mostram diferentes formas de refrescar o interior. O design bioclimático facilita a evacuação de ar quente para fora da casa.

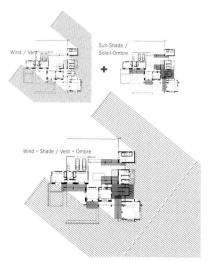

Wind / Vent

Sun-Shade / Soleil-Ombre

Wind + Shade / Vent + Ombre

4.3. Creation of shade

The positioning of a house towards the south may be a good idea for the winter months but to escape the heat in the summer it is necessary to prevent the sun's rays from entering the house. Common systems are the slope of the roof and eaves, vegetation and awnings, umbrellas, curtains and blinds. In short, the aim is to avoid using air conditioning as it consumes energy.

Studying the breezes and the effect of the sun's rays defined the position of this house. The built-in overhangs give shade in the summer.

4.3. Schattenbildung

Die Ausrichtung eines Hauses nach Süden hin kann für den Winter eine gute Lösung sein. In den Sommermonaten müssen aber das Eindringen der Sonnenstrahlen und die dadurch erzeugte Hitze vermieden werden. Die gebräuchlichen Methoden sind in diesem Fall die Neigung der Dächer und Vordächer, Vegetation, Markisen, Sonnenschirme, Gardinen und Rollläden. Definitiv geht es dabei darum, den Einsatz der Klimaanlage zu vermeiden, da sie Energie verbraucht.

Die Untersuchung der Luftströmungen und des Einfalls der Sonnenstrahlen hat die Ausrichtung des Hauses bestimmt. Die gebauten Markisen bieten im Sommer Schatten.

4.3. Faire de l'ombre

L'orientation au sud peut être une bonne solution l'hiver. Toutefois, pour ne pas souffrir de la chaleur estivale, il faut empêcher les rayons du soleil de pénétrer dans la maison l'été. En général, on a recours à la pente du toit et à la pose d'auvents, à la végétation et aux volets, stores, rideaux et persiennes. Il s'agit de tout faire pour éviter la climatisation, gourmande en énergie.

L'orientation de la maison a été décidée après une étude des courants d'air et de l'incidence des rayons du soleil. Les avant-toits font de l'ombre l'été.

4.3. Schaduwvorming

De ligging van een huis op het zuiden kan in de winter een goede oplossing zijn, maar om de hitte tijdens warme maanden tegen te gaan, is het noodzakelijk om te voorkomen dat de zonnestralen naar binnen schijnen. De gebruikelijke systemen zijn de inclinatie van daken en overstekende dakranden, planten en

* 4.3

zonneschermen, parasols, gordijnen en jaloezieën. Kortom, het gaat erom het gebruik van airconditioning te vermijden omdat zij energie verbruikt.
De bestudering van luchtstromingen en de inval van zonnestralen heeft de ligging van het huis bepaald. De gemetselde luifels zorgen in de zomer voor schaduw.

4.3. Creación de sombras
La orientación de una casa hacia el sur puede ser una buena solución para el invierno pero, para evitar el calor durante los meses cálidos, es necesario evitar que los rayos de sol entren en la casa. Los sistemas habituales son la inclinación de los tejados y los aleros, la vegetación y los toldos, sombrillas, cortinas y persianas. En definitiva, se trata de evitar el uso del aire acondicionado, pues consume energía.
El estudio de las corrientes de aire y de la incidencia de los rayos de sol ha definido la orientación de la casa. Las marquesinas de obra proporcionan sombra en verano.

4.3. Creazione di ombre
L'orientamento di una casa verso sud può essere una buona soluzione per l'inverno però, per evitare il caldo durante i mesi caldi, è necessario fare in modo che i raggi del sole non entrino in casa. I sistemi abituali sono l'inclinazione dei tetti, i cornicioni, la vegetazione, le tende solari, gli ombrelloni, i tendaggi e le persiane. In definitiva, si tratta di evitare l'uso dell'aria condizionata dato che consuma energia.
Lo studio delle correnti d'aria e dell'incidenza dei raggi solari ha definito l'orientamento della casa. Le tettoie in muratura danno ombra durante l'estate.

4.3. Criação de sombras
A orientação de uma casa para sul pode ser uma boa solução para o Inverno mas, para evitar o calor durante os meses quentes, é necessário evitar que os raios de sol entrem na casa. Os sistemas habituais são a inclinação dos telhados e os beirais, a vegetação e os toldos, guarda-sóis, cortinas e persianas. Em resumo, trata-se de evitar o uso do ar condicionado, pois consome energia.
O estudo das correntes de ar e da incidência dos raios de sol definiu a orientação da casa. As coberturas de alvenaria proporcionam sombra no Verão.

4.4. Vegetation
Vegetation is an essential element in bioclimatic design. Gardens cool the air and trees offer shade and protection from the wind. Evergreen trees are recommended as they give shade in the summer and allow the sun in during the winter. Green roofs increase insulation, manage rainwater, increase soundproofing and reduce the urban heat island effect.
Membranes on green roofs insulate and allow water drainage. Native plants, well-adapted to the area's climate should be planted.

4.4. Vegetation
Die Vegetation stellt ein unbedingt notwendiges Element beim bioklimatischen Design dar. Gärten dienen zur Luftabkühlung und Bäume spenden Schatten und Windschutz. Es wird empfohlen, immergrüne Bäume zu pflanzen, da sie im Sommer Schatten spenden und im Winter die Sonne durchlassen. Begrünte Dächer erhöhen die Hausisolierung, verarbeiten das Regenwasser, verbessern die Lärmisolierung und senken die Wärmeinselwirkung.
Die Membranen der begrünten Dächer isolieren und ermöglichen die Wasserdrainage. Es sollen bodenständige Pflanzen angepflanzt werden, die an das Klima der Region angepasst sind.

© Scott McGlashan   *4.4

4.4. Végétation
La végétation est un élément indispensable de la conception bioclimatique. Les jardins rafraîchissent l'air ; les arbres apportent ombre et protection contre le vent. Il est conseillé de planter des arbres à feuilles caduques, qui font de l'ombre l'été et laissent passer le soleil l'hiver. Les toitures végétales améliorent l'isolation de la maison, participent à la gestion des eaux de pluie, renforcent l'isolation acoustique et réduisent l'effet île de chaleur.
Les feuilles isolantes placées sous les toitures végétalisées isolent et facilitent l'écoulement de l'eau. Il faut planter des variétés endémiques adaptées au climat local.

4.4. Planten
Planten vormen een onontbeerlijk element van het bioklimatisch design. Tuinen verfrissen de lucht en bomen zorgen voor schaduw en bescherming tegen de wind. Aanbevolen wordt om zomergroene loofbomen te planten die in de zomer voor schaduw zorgen en in de winter de zon doorlaten. Groendaken verhogen

de isolatie van het huis, regelen het regenwater, verbeteren de geluidsisolatie en verminderen het hitte-eilandeffect.

De membranen van groendaken isoleren en bevorderen de afwatering. Er moeten bij het plaatselijke klimaat passende autochtone plantensoorten worden geplant.

4.4. Vegetación

La vegetación es un elemento imprescindible del diseño bioclimático. Los jardines refrescan el aire y los árboles proporcionan sombra y refugio del viento. Se recomienda plantar árboles de hoja perenne, que den sombra en verano y dejen pasar el sol en invierno. Las cubiertas vegetales aumentan el aislamiento de la casa, gestionan el agua de lluvia, mejoran el aislamiento acústico y disminuyen el efecto de isla de calor.

Las membranas de las cubiertas ajardinadas aíslan y permiten el drenaje del agua. Se deben plantar especies autóctonas adaptadas al clima de la zona.

4.4. Vegetazione

La vegetazione è un elemento imprescindibile del progetto bioclimatico. I giardini rinfrescano l'aria e gli alberi offrono ombra e riparano dal vento. Si raccomanda piantare alberi di foglia perenne che possano dare ombra durante l'estate e che lascino filtrare il sole durante l'inverno. Le coperture vegetali aumentano l'isolamento della casa, gestiscono l'acqua piovana, migliorano l'isolamento acustico e diminuiscono la formazione dell'isola di calore.

Le membrane delle coperture verdi sono isolanti e consentono il drenaggio dell'acqua. È doveroso piantare specie autoctone adattate al clima della zona.

4.4. Vegetação

A vegetação é um elemento imprescindível do design bioclimático. Os jardins refrescam o ar e as árvores proporcionam sombra e protecção contra o vento. É recomendável plantar árvores de folha perene, que façam sombra no Verão e deixem passar o sol no Inverno. As coberturas vegetais aumentam o isolamento da casa, gerem a água da chuva, melhoram o isolamento acústico e diminuem o efeito de ilha de calor.

As membranas das coberturas ajardinadas isolam e permitem a drenagem da água. Devem plantar-se espécies autóctones adaptadas ao clima da zona.

4.5. Insulation: glass, walls, etc.

Good insulation is the best way to save energy and heat or cool a house. If windows and doors are not well-sealed, heat or cool air escapes and energy is wasted. Installing windows with a thermal break or insulated walls maintains indoor temperature. Double or triple glazing has improved window efficiency. The air chamber between the glass, filled with inert gas, keeps the temperature stable.

A. Double or triple glazing avoids unwanted thermal increases.
B. Low-e glass reduces heat from sunlight and allows the entrance of natural light (1- 30% of solar heat. 2- 70% of light via the glass).

4.5. Isolierung: Scheiben, Wände, usw.

Eine gute Isolierung ist der beste Weg, Energie bei der Klimatisierung eines Wohnhauses zu sparen. Sind Fenster oder Türen undicht, entweicht Wärme oder Kälte nach draußen und es wird Energie verschwendet. Der Einbau von Fenstern mit Wärmebrückenunterbrechung oder Isolierwänden erhält die Innentemperatur. Doppelt oder dreifach verglaste Scheiben haben die Leistung der Fenster verbessert. Die mit Edelgasen gefüllte Luftkammer zwischen den Scheiben ermöglicht stabile Temperaturen.

A. Doppelte oder dreifache Verglasung verhindert unerwünschte Wärmeaufnahmen.
B. Low-e-Scheiben senken die Sonnenaufnahme und erlauben den Lichteinfall (1- 30 % Sonnenaufnahme. 2- 70 % Licht durch das Glas).

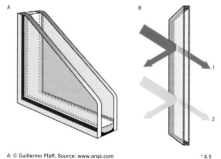

A
B
1
2

A: © Guillermo Pfaff. Source: www.arqa.com
B: © Guillermo Pfaff. Source: www.metaefficient.com

*4.5

4.5. Isolation : verres, murs, etc.

Une bonne isolation est la meilleure façon d'économiser l'énergie tout en conservant une température agréable dans un logement. Si portes et fenêtres ne sont pas étanches, la chaleur ou le froid peuvent s'échapper à l'extérieur entrainant un gaspillage d'énergie. L'installation de fenêtres avec rupture de pont thermique et la pose de doublages pour isoler les murs aident à maintenir une température égale à l'intérieur. Les doubles et triples vitrages ont amélioré le rendement des fenêtres. Quand le vide d'air entre les deux parois de verre est rempli de gaz nobles, il est encore plus facile de conserver une température stable.

A. Pendant les grosses chaleurs, les verres doubles ou triples évitent que la température monte trop à l'intérieur.
B. Les verres basse-émission bloquent la chaleur des rayons solaires tout en laissant passer la lumière (1- 30 % de gain solaire. 2- 70 % de la lumière traverse la vitre).

4.5. Isolatie: glazen, wanden, etc.
Een goede isolatie is de beste manier om energie te besparen voor de klimaatregeling van een woning. Als ramen en deuren niet luchtdicht zijn, ontsnapt warmte of kou naar buiten en wordt energie verspild. De installatie van ramen met koudebrugonderbrekingen of isolerende wanden handhaven de binnentemperatuur. Dubbele of driedubbele beglazing verbetert het rendement van de ramen. De luchtkamer tussen de glasplaten, gevuld met edelgassen, zorgt voor een stabiele temperatuur.
A. Dubbele en driedubbele glazen verhinderen ongewenste warmtewinsten.
B. Low-e glas reduceert de zonneopbrengst en maakt de inval van licht mogelijk (1- 30% zonneopbrengst. 2- 70% lichtinval via de ruit).

4.5. Aislamiento: cristales, paredes, etc.
Un buen aislamiento es la mejor forma de ahorrar energía para climatizar una vivienda. Si las ventanas o las puertas no son estancas, el calor o el frío se escapan al exterior y se malgasta energía. La instalación de ventanas con rotura de puente térmico o las paredes aislantes mantienen la temperatura interior. Las cristaleras de doble e triple vidrio han mejorado el rendimiento de las ventanas. La cámara de aire entre los cristales, rellenada con gases nobles, facilita la temperatura estable.
A. Los cristales dobles o triples evitan ganancias térmicas indeseadas.
B. Los cristales Low-e reducen la ganancia solar y permiten la entrada de luz (1- 30% de ganancia solar. 2- 70% de luz a través del vidrio).

4.5. Isolamento termico: vetri, pareti, ecc.
Un buon isolamento termico è la migliore maniera di risparmiare energia necessaria per climatizzare un'abitazione. Se le finestre o le porte non sono a tenuta, si produrrà una dispersione termica con conseguente spreco d'energia. L'installazione di finestre con rottura di ponte termico o di pareti isolanti mantengono stabile la temperatura interna. Le vetrate a doppio e triplo vetro hanno migliorato la resa delle finestre. La camera d'aria tra i vetri, intercapedine che contiene gas nobile, facilita la stabilizzazione della temperatura.
A. I vetri doppi o tripli evitano i guadagni di calore indesiderati.
B. I vetri low-e riducono il guadagno solare e consentono l'entrata della luce (1- 30% di guadagno solare. 2- 70% di luce attraverso il vetro).

4.5. Isolamento: vidros, paredes, etc.
Um bom isolamento é a melhor forma de poupar energia para climatizar uma habitação. Se as janelas ou as portas não garantirem um bom isolamento, o calor ou o frio saem para o exterior e desperdiça-se energia. A instalação de janelas com ruptura de ponte térmica ou as paredes isolantes mantêm a temperatura interior. As vidraças de vidro duplo e triplo melhoraram o rendimento das janelas. A câmara de ar entre os vidros, preenchida com gases nobres, facilita uma temperatura estável.
A. Os vidros duplos ou triplos evitam cargas térmicas indesejadas. B. Os vidros low-e reduzem a carga solar e permitem a entrada de luz (1- 30% de carga solar. 2- 70% de luz através do vidro).

*4.6

4.6. Lighting: ways to save
Lighting systems should respect the environment and natural light should be encouraged with the use of; glass walls, skylights and even the installation of solar tubes. Using low consumption light bulbs and fluorescent bulbs or LEDs is recommended. A variety can be found on the market and they offer different kinds of cooler or warmer light.
Design need not suffer for the sake of efficiency. There are more and more low consumption light bulbs available which suit all kinds of interior decoration.

4.6. Beleuchtung: Einsparsysteme
Die Beleuchtungssysteme müssen umweltfreundlich sein. Der Tageslichteinfall soll durch den Bau von Glaswänden, Dachluken und sogar Solarrohren gefördert werden. Es wird außerdem empfohlen, Glühbirnen oder Leuchtstoffröhren mit niedrigem Verbrauch oder LED-Lampen zu verwenden. Auf dem Markt sind Modelle erhältlich, die sich allen Stilrichtungen anpassen und unterschiedliche Lichtarten - kälter oder wärmer - abgeben.
Das Design muss kein Hindernis für die Effizienz sein. Es gibt immer mehr Glühbirnenmodelle mit niedrigem Verbrauch, die sich alle Einrichtungsstile anpassen.

4.6. Éclairage : moyens pour économiser
Les modes d'éclairage doivent être respectueux du milieu. Il faut préférer l'éclairage naturel, par exemple en construisant des murs ou cloisons en verre ou à claire-voie ou encore en installant des tubes solaires. Il est

également recommandé d'utiliser des ampoules fluorescentes basse consommation ou des éclairages à leds. Il existe aujourd'hui sur le marché de nombreux modèles qui s'adaptent à tous les styles et émettent des lumières plus ou moins chaudes ou froides.

L'élégance n'est pas incompatible avec l'efficacité. Il y a de plus en plus de modèles d'ampoules basse consommation qui s'adaptent à tous les styles de luminaires.

4.6. Verlichting: spaarsystemen

Verlichtingssystemen moeten milieuvriendelijk zijn. Natuurlijke verlichting moet bevorderd worden: er kunnen glaswanden, dakramen en zelfs zonnebuizen worden geïnstalleerd. Eveneens wordt het gebruik van spaarlampen of ledlampen aanbevolen. Er bestaan modellen op de markt die bij elke stijl passen en die verschillende soorten killer of warmer licht uitstralen.

Design en efficiëntie kunnen samengaan. Er zijn telkens meer spaarlampen die bij elke decoratiestijl passen.

4.6. Iluminación: sistemas de ahorro

Los sistemas de iluminación deben ser respetuosos con el medio ambiente. Se debe potenciar la iluminación natural: se pueden construir paredes de cristal, claraboyas e incluso instalar tubos solares. También es recomendable utilizar bombillas o fluorescentes de bajo consumo o luces led. En el mercado existen modelos que se adaptan a todos los estilos y que emiten diferentes tipos de luz, más fría o cálida.

El diseño no está reñido con la eficiencia. Cada vez existen más modelos de bombillas de bajo consumo que se adaptan a cualquier estilo decorativo.

4.6. Illuminazione: sistema di risparmio

I sistema d'illuminazione devono essere rispettosi dell'ambiente. Si deve potenziare l'illuminazione naturale: si possono costruire pareti in vetro, lucernari e addirittura installare tubi solari. È raccomandabile, inoltre, l'utilizzo di lampadine o lampade fluorescenti a basso consumo o di luci Led. Il mercato offre modelli che si adeguano a tutti gli stili e che emettono diversi tipi di luce, più fredda o più calda.

Il design non va a detrimento dell'efficienza. Sul mercato è possibile trovare sempre più modelli di lampadine a basso consumo che si adattano a qualunque stile decorativo.

4.6. Iluminação: sistemas de poupança

Os sistemas de iluminação devem respeitar o ambiente. Deve-se reforçar a iluminação natural: podem construir-se paredes de vidro, clarabóias e até instalar-se tubos solares. Também é recomendável a utilização de lâmpadas fluorescentes de baixo consumo ou de luzes Led. Existem no mercado modelos que se adaptam a todos os estilos e que emitem diferentes tipos de luz, mais fria ou cálida.

O design não é incompatível com a eficiência. Cada vez existem mais modelos de lâmpadas de baixo consumo que se adaptam a qualquer estilo decorativo.

5. ACTIVE SYSTEMS

Active systems are those which generate energy from renewable sources: solar, aeolic, geothermal, etc. Clean or alternative energies do not produce CO_2 emissions and are inexhaustible.

5. AKTIVE SYSTEME

Unter aktiven Systemen versteht man solche, die Energie aus erneuerbaren Quellen wie Solar-, Wind-, Geothermiequellen usw. erzeugen. Diese sogenannten sauberen oder alternativen Energien verursachen keine CO_2-Abgaben und sind unerschöpflich.

5. SYSTÈMES ACTIFS

Les systèmes actifs sont ceux qui utilisent les énergies renouvelables - solaire, éolien ou géothermie, etc. Les énergies propres ou alternatives ne dégagent pas de CO_2 et sont inépuisables.

5. ACTIEVE SYSTEMEN

Actieve systemen zijn systemen die vanuit hernieuwbare bronnen energie opwekken: o.a. zonne-, wind- en geothermische energie. Schone of alternatieve energieën produceren geen CO_2-uitstoot en zijn onuitputtelijk.

5. SISTEMAS ACTIVOS

Los sistemas activos son aquellos que generan energía a partir de fuentes renovables: solar, eólica, geotérmica, etc. Las energías limpias o alternativas no generan emisiones de CO_2 y son inagotables.

5. SISTEMI ATTIVI

I sistemi attivi sono quelli che generano energia avvalendosi di fonti rinnovabili: solare, eolica, geotermica, ecc. Le energie pulite o alternative non generano emissioni di CO_2 e sono inesauribili.

5. SISTEMAS ACTIVOS

Os sistemas activos são aqueles que geram energia a partir de fontes renováveis: solar, eólica, geotérmica, etc. As energias limpas ou alternativas não geram emissões de CO_2 e são inesgotáveis.

© John Swain   * 5.1

5.1. Solar panels

There are basically two types of solar panels: photovoltaic, which convert solar energy into electricity, and thermal, which heat the water in its pipes for heating and hot water. A calculation of the total solar panel surface should be made to ensure there is enough electricity and heating for each family. It is advisable to check if government subsidies exist for these installations.
The working life of photovoltaic solar panels is about 20-30 years, enough to cover the cost of the investment.

5.1. Solarplatten

Grundsätzlich gibt es zwei Arten an Solarplatten: Fotovoltaikplatten, welche die Sonnenenergie in Strom umwandeln, und Wärmeplatten, welche das in Rohren vorhandene Wasser für Heizung und Duschen heizen. Es wird empfohlen, die Solarplattenfläche, die für den Strom- und Heizungsbedarf der einzelnen Familien erforderlich ist, zu berechnen. Zudem sollte man sich erkundigen, ob die Regierungen Förderungen für diese Installationen anbieten.
Die Lebensdauer der Fotovoltaiksolarplatten beträgt 20 - 30 Jahre und ist somit ausreichend, um die Investition abschreiben zu können.

5.1. Panneaux solaires

Il existe deux sortes de panneaux solaires : les panneaux photovoltaïques, qui convertissent l'énergie solaire en électricité, et les panneaux thermiques, qui chauffent l'eau contenue dans les tuyaux pour le chauffage et la douche. Il est prudent de calculer la surface de panneaux solaires nécessaires pour répondre au besoin en électricité de chaque famille et de vérifier les derniers dispositifs législatifs en matière de subventions ou d'aides fiscales avant de commander une installation.
La durée de vie des panneaux solaires photovoltaïques est de 20 à 30 ans, ce qui suffit pour amortir son investissement.

5.1. Zonnepanelen

Er zijn in wezen twee soorten zonnepanelen: de fotovoltaïsche, die zonne-energie in elektrische energie omzetten, en de thermische, die het water in de verwarmingsbuizen en douches verwarmen. Het is raadzaam om de oppervlakte van de zonnepanelen die nodig zijn voor het stroom- en verwarmingsverbruik van het gezin te berekenen. Aanbevolen wordt om te informeren of regeringen subsidies voor deze installaties verlenen.
De levensduur van fotovoltaïsche zonnepanelen bedraagt ongeveer 20-30 jaar, genoeg om de investering terug te verdienen.

5.1. Placas solares

Básicamente existen de dos tipos de placas solares: las fotovoltaicas, que convierten la energía solar en eléctrica, y las térmicas, que calientan el agua contenida en los tubos para calefacción y duchas. Es recomendable realizar un cálculo de la superficie de placas solares que se necesitará para el consumo de electricidad y calefacción de cada familia. Se recomienda consultar si los gobiernos conceden subvenciones a estas instalaciones.
La vida útil de las placas solares fotovoltaicas es de unos 20-30 años, suficiente para amortizar la inversión.

5.1. Placche solari

Basicamente esistono due tipi di placche solari: quelle fotovoltaiche, che trasformano l'energia solare in elettrica, e quelle termiche, che riscaldano l'acqua contenuta nei tubi per il riscaldamento e le docce. È raccomandabile realizzare un calcolo della superficie di placche solari di cui si ha bisogno per il consumo d'elettricità e per il sistema di riscaldamento di ogni famiglia. Si raccomanda di accertarsi dell'esistenza d'eventuali sovvenzioni tese a fomentare la diffusione di queste installazioni.
La vita utile delle placche solari fotovoltaiche è di circa 20-30 anni, un periodo sufficiente per ammortizzare l'investimento.

5.1. Painéis solares

Basicamente existem dois tipos de painéis solares: os fotovoltaicos, que convertem a energia solar em eléctrica, e os térmicos, que aquecem a água contida nos tubos para o aquecimento e duches. É recomendável realizar um cálculo da superfície de painéis solares necessária para o consumo de electricidade e aquecimento de cada família. É recomendável saber se os governos concedem subsídios para estas instalações.

A vida útil dos painéis solares fotovoltaicos é de cerca de 20-30 anos, suficiente para amortizar o investimento.

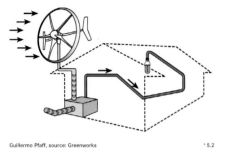

Guillermo Pfaff, source: Greenworks   ⁎ 5.2

5.2. Aeolic micro-generators

Another system which generates electricity is the aeolic micro-generator. There is not one single kind, but in general they are similar to big aeolic turbines. Their sole dependence on the wind means they should be installed in areas with electricity or to complement other sources of electricity. They can generate 30% of a household's energy and do so with less visual impact, lower costs, more efficiency and better sustainability.

Most of these micro-generators have a horizontal axis and three blades. Vertical- axis generators also exist and have less acoustic impact.

5.2. Mikrowindenergieanlagen

Ein weiteres System zur Energieerzeugung sind Mikrowindenergieanlagen. Hierbei gibt es keine Einzeleinstufung, aber grundsätzlich ähneln sie den großen Windenergieturbinen. Ihre Abhängigkeit vom Wind rät dazu, sie in Gebieten mit Stromversorgung oder als Ergänzung weiterer Stromquellen zu installieren. Sie können 30 % des Energieverbrauchs eines Haushalts mit geringerer optischer Auswirkung, niedrigeren Kosten, höherer Effizienz und längerer Nachhaltigkeit erzeugen.

Die meisten dieser Mikrowindenergieanlagen bestehen aus einer waagerechten Achse und drei Blättern. Es gibt auch Energieanlagen mit senkrechter Achse und geringerer akustischer Auswirkung.

5.2. Éoliennes

Le recours aux éoliennes est un autre moyen de produire de l'électricité. Il en existe plusieurs types mais toutes fonctionnent sur le même principe que les grandes éoliennes verticales. Comme elles ont besoin de vent pour fonctionner, il est préférable de disposer d'une autre source d'électricité et de les utiliser en complément. Elles peuvent fournir jusqu'à 30 % de l'énergie consommée par chaque foyer. Contrairement aux idées reçues, elles se voient très peu, sont peu onéreuses, très efficaces et incarnent la notion de durable à la perfection.

La majorité des microgénérateurs éoliens ont un axe horizontal et trois pales. Il existe aussi des aérogénérateurs à axe vertical, ayant un impact acoustique moindre.

5.2. Microwindgenerators

Een ander systeem dat elektriciteit opwekt zijn microwindgenerators. Er bestaat geen unieke classificatie, maar over het algemeen zijn het machines die op de grote windmolens lijken. Vanwege de afhankelijkheid van de wind, wordt aanbevolen om ze in zones met stroomvoorziening te installeren of ze als aanvulling op andere elektriciteitsbronnen te gebruiken. Ze kunnen 30% van de door elk huishouden verbruikte energie produceren en doen dit met een kleiner visueel effect, lagere kosten, een hogere efficiëntie en een langere duurzaamheid.

De meeste van deze microgenerators hebben een horizontale as en drie schoepen. Ook zijn er generators met een verticale as die een lager geluidsimpact hebben.

5.2. Microgeneradores eólicos

Otro de los sistemas que generan electricidad son los microgeneradores eólicos. No existe una clasificación única, pero en general son máquinas similares a las grandes turbinas eólicas. Su dependencia del viento recomienda que se instalen en zonas con suministro eléctrico o que sean un complemento a otras fuentes de electricidad. Pueden producir el 30% de la energía que consume un hogar y lo hacen con menor impacto visual, menores costes, mayor eficiencia y mayor sostenibilidad.

La mayoría de estos microgeneradores son de eje horizontal y de tres paletas. También existen generadores de eje vertical, de menor impacto acústico.

5.2. Microgeneratori eolici

Un altro sistema che genera elettricità è quello rappresentato dai microgeneratori eolici. Non esiste una classificazione unica però, in generale, sono macchine simili alle grandi turbine eoliche. La loro dipendenza dal vento ne consiglia l'installazione nelle zone con somministrazione d'energia elettrica o come alternativa

complementare ad altre fonti di elettricità. I microgeneratori eolici possono produrre il 30% dell'energia che consuma ogni casa con un impatto visivo ed un costo minore ma una maggiore efficienza e sostenibilità.
La maggior parte di questi microgeneratori sono ad asse orizzontale e a tre pale. Esistono anche generatori ad asse verticale, dal minore impatto acustico.

5.2. Microgeradores eólicos
Outro dos sistemas que geram electricidade são os microgeradores eólicos. Não existe uma classificação única, mas em geral são máquinas similares às grandes turbinas eólicas. A sua dependência do vento torna recomendável que se instalem em zonas com abastecimento eléctrico ou que sejam um complemento a outras fontes de electricidade. Podem produzir 30% da energia que cada lar consome e fazem-no com menor impacto visual, menores custos, maior eficiência e maior sustentabilidade.
A maioria destes microgeradores são de eixo horizontal e de três pás. Também existem geradores de eixo vertical, com menor impacto acústico.

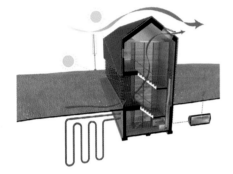

* 5.3

5.3. Geothermal energy
Geothermal energy is produced by using underground heat, which gives back or extracts heat thanks to buried collectors in which water and glycol circulate. To cool a building, the system transmits the surplus heat to the ground. In winter, the geothermal installation heats the building with the reverse process. It can be installed in any building, although it is not available worldwide, and avoids energy dependency. Waste is negligible and their environmental impact minimal.
The house designed by Studio 804 examines geothermal energy; a silent energy which is compatible with other renewable ones.

5.3. Energie aus Erdwärme
Energie aus Erdwärme wird durch Nutzung der Wärme des Untergrunds gewonnen. Dabei wird Wärme vom Unterboden abgegeben oder dank eingegrabener Sammelleitungen, durch die Wasser mit Glykol fließt, entnommen. Zur Abkühlung eines Gebäudes überträgt dieses System die überschüssige Wärme in den Unterboden. Im Winter wird das Gebäude von der Geothermieanlage mit dem umgekehrten Vorgang beheizt. Sie sind zwar nicht überall verfügbar, können aber in allen Gebäuden installiert werden und vermeiden dessen Energieabhängigkeit. Die Abfälle sind minimal und verursachen eine geringe Umweltauswirkung.
Das von Studio 804 entworfene Haus nutzt Energie aus Erdwärme. Dabei handelt es sich um leise Energie, die mit anderen erneuerbaren Energien gekoppelt werden kann.

5.3. Énergie géothermique
L'énergie géothermique est celle produite grâce à la chaleur accumulée dans le sous-sol. En fonction des besoins, on peut produire de la chaleur ou l'évacuer à l'aide de collecteurs enterrés dans lesquels circule un mélange d'eau et de glycol. Pour refroidir un bâtiment, le liquide caloporteur achemine la chaleur à l'extérieur dans le sous-sol. En hiver, l'installation géothermique permet de chauffer en puisant la chaleur du sous-sol pour l'amener à l'intérieur. Il est toujours possible d'équiper une maison en géothermie mais cette technologie n'est pas encore disponible partout dans le monde. Elle réduit la dépendance énergétique et son impact sur l'environnement est très faible puisqu'elle ne génère qu'un minimum de déchets.
Pour faire les plans ce cette maison, Studio 804 a envisagé l'énergie géothermique, une énergie silencieuse et compatible avec les autres énergies renouvelables.

5.3. Geothermische energie
Geothermische energie wordt verkregen uit de inwendige warmte van de aarde, die dankzij ondergrondse collectoren waardoor water met glycol circuleert kan worden benut. Om een gebouw te koelen draagt het systeem de overtollige warmte over op de aarde. In de winter verwarmt de geothermische installatie het gebouw in een omgekeerd proces. Het kan in elk gebouw worden geïnstalleerd, hoewel het niet overal ter wereld beschikbaar is, en vermijdt de energieafhankelijkheid. Dit systeem brengt minimaal afval voort en heeft een beperkt milieu-effect.
Het door Studio 804 ontworpen huis is bedacht op geothermische energie, een stille energie die compatibel is met andere hernieuwbare energieën.

5.3. Energía geotérmica
La energía geotérmica se consigue aprovechando el calor del subsuelo. La climatización geotérmica cede o extrae calor gracias a unos colectores enterrados por los que circula agua con glicol. Para refrigerar un edificio, el sistema transmite el calor excedente al subsuelo. En invierno, la instalación geotérmica calienta el edificio con el proceso inverso. Puede instalarse en cualquier edificio, aunque no está disponible en

todo el mundo, y evita la dependencia energética. Los residuos son mínimos y ocasionan un impacto medioambiental reducido.

La casa diseñada por Studio 804 contempla la energía geotérmica, una energía silenciosa y compatible con otras renovables.

5.3. Energia geotermica

L'energia geotermica si ottiene sfruttando la temperatura immagazzinata nel sottosuolo che viene estratta grazie a dei collettori interrati nei quali circola dell'acqua con glicole etilenico. Per refrigerare un edificio il sistema trasmette il calore in eccesso al sottosuolo mentre, durante l'inverno, l'installazione geotermica scalda l'edificio con il processo inverso. Questo sistema può essere installato in qualunque edificio, sebbene non sia disponibile in ogni parte del mondo, permettendo di evitare la dipendenza energetica. I residui sono minimi e producono un impatto ambientale ridotto.

La casa progettata da Studio 804 prevede un'installazione geotermica che consente lo sfruttamento di un'energia silenziosa e compatibile con altre energie rinnovabili.

5.3. Energia geotérmica

A energia geotérmica consegue-se, aproveitando o calor do subsolo, o qual cede ou absorve calor graças a uns colectores enterrados pelos quais circula água com glicol. Para refrescar um edifício, o sistema transmite o calor excedente ao subsolo. No Inverno, a instalação geotérmica aquece o edifício com o processo inverso. Pode instalar-se em qualquer edifício, embora não esteja disponível em todo o mundo, e evita a dependência energética. Os resíduos são mínimos e causam um impacto ambiental reduzido.

A casa projectada pelo Studio 804 contempla a energia geotérmica, uma energia silenciosa e compatível com outras renováveis.

*5.4

5.4. Biomass

Biomass is an organic material produced from a biological process and used as a source of energy. Various types exist: natural biomass, which is produced by nature without man's intervention; residual biomass, made of waste generated from agricultural, farming and forest activity and lastly one from crops. The most appropriate one for home use is direct combustion in wood or *pellets* stoves.

Pellet is a type of granulated fuel made from waste wood such as wood shavings, sawdust or wood chips. It is a 100% biodegradable material.

5.4. Biomasse

Bei Biomasse handelt es sich um organisches Material, das bei einem biologischen Ablauf entsteht und als Energiequelle eingesetzt wird. Es gibt unterschiedliche Arten, wie natürliche Biomasse, die von der Natur selbst ohne Eingriff der Menschen erzeugt wird, Biomasse aus Abfällen, die bei land- und forstwirtschaftlichen sowie Viehzuchttätigkeiten entsteht oder Biomasse aus dem Energiepflanzenanbau. Die für ein Wohnhaus geeignetste Variante ist die Biomassendirektverbrennung in Holz- oder Pelletöfen.

Pellets sind eine Art körniger Brennstoff, der aus Holzresten wie Spänen, Sägemehl oder Splittern hergestellt wird. Hierbei handelt es sich 100 % biologisch abbaubares Material.

5.4. Biomasse

La biomasse est la matière organique résultant d'un processus de décomposition biologique qui est utilisée comme source d'énergie. Il en existe plusieurs sortes : la biomasse naturelle, produite par la nature sans intervention humaine, la biomasse résiduelle, qui est composée des déchets provenant de l'agriculture, de l'élevage et de l'exploitation forestière, et la biomasse provenant de cultures énergétiques. La méthode la mieux adaptée pour chauffer un logement est la combustion directe de biomasse, dans un poêle à bois ou en *granulé*.

Le granulé est un combustible fabriqué avec des déchets de bois, copeaux, sciure ou éclats. C'est un matériau 100 % biodégradable.

5.4. Biomassa

Biomassa is de organische materie die tijdens een biologisch proces voortgebracht en als energiebron gebruikt wordt. Er bestaan diverse soorten: natuurlijke biomassa, die de natuur zonder tussenkomst van de mens levert, residuale biomassa, die bestaat uit bij landbouw-, veeteelt- en bosbouwactiviteiten voortgebracht afval, en de biomassa afkomstig van energieteelt. Het systeem dat het best in een woning kan worden gebruikt is de directe verbranding van biomassa in kachels voor brandhout of *pellets*.

Pellet is een korrelige brandstof gemaakt van houtresten zoals spaanders, zaagsel of schaafsel. Het gaat om een 100% biologisch afbreekbaar materiaal.

5.4. Biomasa

La biomasa es la materia orgánica originada en un proceso biológico que se utiliza como fuente de energía. Existen varios tipos: la biomasa natural, la que produce la naturaleza sin intervención del hombre; la residual, que está compuesta por residuos generados en actividades agrícolas, ganaderas y forestales, y la procedente de cultivos energéticos. Lo más recomendable en una vivienda es la combustión directa de biomasa en estufas de leña o de *pellets*.

*El pellet *es un tipo de combustible granulado fabricado con excedentes de madera, como virutas, serrín o astillas. Se trata de un material 100% biodegradable.*

5.4. Biomassa

Per biomassa s'intende la materia organica originata da un processo biologico ed utilizzata come fonte d'energia. Esistono vari tipi di biomassa: quella naturale, prodotta dalla natura senza l'intervento dell'uomo, quella residuale, composta da residui generati dalle attività agricole, allevamento e forestali, e quella proveniente da colture energetiche. Quella più facilmente utilizzabile in un'abitazione è senz'altro la combustione diretta di biomasse in stufe a legna o a *pellet*.

Il pellet è un combustibile granulare prodotto con eccedenti del legno, come scaglie, segatura o trucioli. Si tratta di un materiale biodegradabile al 100%.

5.4. Biomassa

A biomassa é a matéria orgânica originada por um processo biológico que se utiliza como fonte de energia. Existem vários tipos: a biomassa natural, que é produzida pela natureza sem intervenção do homem; a residual, que é composta por resíduos gerados em actividades agrícolas, florestais e na criação animal, e a procedente de culturas energéticas. A que melhor se pode utilizar numa habitação é a combustão directa de biomassa em recuperadores a lenha ou de *pellets*.

O pellet é um tipo de combustível granulado fabricado com excedentes de madeira, como aparas, serradura ou estilha. Trata-se de um material 100% biodegradável.

© Obie Bowman

* 5.5

5.5. Out of the grid

This expression is used to describe homes which only use clean electric energy and are not connected to a conventional electricity grid. The energy supply is via a combination of active and passive systems. These homes typically also have their own rainwater collection system and are totally self-sufficient, thus showing that sustainable architecture is possible.

Obie G. Bowman's cabin is an example of a "disconnected" building. It has photovoltaic and thermal solar panels and a rainwater collection system.

5.5. Out of the grid

Diese Bezeichnung wird für Wohnhäuser verwendet, die nur mit sauberer Energie versorgt werden und vom herkömmlichen Stromnetz ausgeschaltet sind. Die Stromversorgung erfolgt anhand einer Kombination aus aktiven und passiven Systemen. Normalerweise besitzen diese Häuser auch ihre eigenen Regenwasserauffangsysteme und sind komplett selbstständig. Damit wird deutlich, dass nachhaltige Architektur möglich ist.

Obige G. Bowmans Hütte ist ein Beispiel für die "abgeschaltete" Bauweise. Sie besitzt Fotovoltaik- und thermische Solarplatten, wie auch ein Auffangsystem für Regenwasser.

5.5. Out of the grid

C'est ainsi que l'on désigne dans les pays anglo-saxons les maisons qui produisent toute l'électricité qui leur est nécessaire et ne sont pas raccordées au réseau. Elles associent des systèmes actifs et passifs. Ces habitations ont généralement aussi leur propre système de collecte des eaux de pluie et sont entièrement autonomes. Elles prouvent que les objectifs d'une architecture respectueuse de l'environnement sont réalisables.

La cabane de Obie G. Bowman est un exemple de construction « déconnectée ». Elle dispose de panneaux solaires photovoltaïques et thermiques et d'un système de collecte des eaux pluviales.

5.5. Out of the grid

Dit begrip wordt gebruikt om te verwijzen naar woningen die zich voorzien van schone elektrische energie en die niet op het conventionele elektriciteitsnet zijn aangesloten. De energievoorziening geschiedt door een combinatie van actieve en passieve systemen. Deze huizen hebben meestal ook hun eigen regenwateropvangsysteem en zijn volledig zelfvoorziend, wat aantoont dat duurzame architectuur mogelijk is.

Het huis van Obie G. Bowman is een voorbeeld van "out of the grid" bouw. Het beschikt over fotovoltaïsche en thermische zonnepanelen en een regenwateropvangsysteem.

5.5. Out of the grid

Esta expresión se utiliza para denominar a las residencias que sólo se abastecen de energía eléctrica limpia y que están desconectadas de la red eléctrica convencional. El abastecimiento energético se realiza con una combinación de sistemas activos y pasivos. Estas casas también acostumbran a tener sus propios sistemas de recolección de agua de lluvia y son completamente autosuficientes, lo que demuestra que la arquitectura sostenible es posible.

La cabaña de Obie G. Bowman es un ejemplo de construcción «desconectada». Tiene placas solares fotovoltaicas y térmicas y un sistema de recolección de aguas pluviales.

5.5. Out of the grid

Con quest'espressione ci si riferisce alle residenze che si riforniscono soltanto di energia elettrica pulita e scollegate dalla rete elettrica convenzionale. Il rifornimento energetico combina l'utilizzo di sistemi attivi e passivi. Queste case dispongono normalmente di un proprio sistema di raccolta dell'acqua piovana e sono completamente autosufficienti, fatto che dimostra che l'architettura sostenibile è possibile.

La capanna di Obie G. Bowman è un esempio di costruzione «scollegata». Ha placche solari fotovoltaiche e termiche ed un sistema di raccolta d'acque piovane.

5.5. Out of the grid

Esta expressão utiliza-se para denominar as residências que apenas consomem energia eléctrica limpa e que não estão ligadas à rede eléctrica convencional. O abastecimento energético realiza-se através de uma combinação de sistemas activos e passivos. Estas casas também costumam ter os seus próprios sistemas de recolha de água da chuva e são completamente auto-suficientes, o que demonstra que a arquitectura sustentável se pode alcançar.

A cabana de Obie G. Bowman é um exemplo de construção «desligada». Tem painéis solares fotovoltaicos e térmicos e um sistema de recolha de águas pluviais.

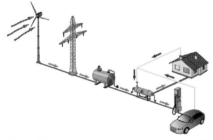

© Guillermo Pfaff
Source: El País, Audi http://blogs.elpais.com/coche-electrico

*5.6

5.6. New systems

Strategies using natural resources are constantly being developed. Audi, for example, is about to unveil its e-gas project which takes advantage of unstorable, surplus wind-generated electricity to obtain hydrogen and, with it, methane. They want to use this gas as fuel for cars and also for heating. It is not 100% emission-free, but it does use surplus aeolic energy and produces less CO_2 than non-renewable energy sources.

CO_2 emitted in methane gas is less than that of petrol or heating oil.

5.6. Neue Systeme

Es werden ständig neue Strategien entwickelt, um natürliche Ressourcen zu nutzen. Audi steht zum Beispiel kurz vor der Umsetzung des e-gas-Projekts. Dabei wird der vom Wind erzeugte Energieüberschuss, der nicht gespeichert werden kann, zur Erzeugung von Wasserstoff und daraus Methan genutzt. Dieses Gas soll als Kraftstoff für das Auto und die Heizung genutzt werden. Es ist nicht 100 % abgabenfrei, verwendet aber die Windenergieüberschüsse und erzeugt weniger CO_2 als nicht erneuerbare Energiequellen.

Das vom Methangas abgegebene CO_2 liegt unter dem von Benzin und Heizöl erzeugten.

5.6. Nouveautés

On ne cesse d'imaginer de nouvelles stratégies qui exploitent les ressources naturelles. Audi, par exemple, est sur le point de mettre en œuvre le projet e-gas, qui consiste à profiter du surcroît d'électricité produit par les éoliennes, que l'on ne sait pas stocker, pour fabriquer de l'hydrogène, puis à partir de l'hydrogène, du méthane. On espère pouvoir utiliser ce gaz comme combustible pour les voitures et le chauffage. Il dégage très peu de CO_2, bien moins que les énergies fossiles, et utilise les excédents de production des éoliennes.

Le méthane dégage moins de CO_2 que les carburants automobiles et le fuel.

5.6. Nieuwe systemen

Er worden voortdurend strategieën ontwikkeld die de natuurlijke hulpbronnen benutten. Audi staat bijvoorbeeld op het punt het e-gas-project in de praktijk te brengen, waarbij het teveel aan elektriciteit dat door de wind wordt voortgebracht en niet kan worden opgeslagen wordt benut om hydrogeen en daarmee methaan te verkrijgen. Dit gas wil men gebruiken als brandstof voor de auto en de verwarming. Het is niet geheel vrij van CO_2-uitstoot, maar gebruikt het overschot van windenergie en brengt minder CO_2 voort dan de niet hernieuwbare energiebronnen.

Methaangas stoot minder CO_2 uit dan benzine of stookolie.

5.6. Nuevos sistemas

Constantemente se desarrollan estrategias que aprovechan los recursos naturales. Así, Audi trabaja en el proyecto e-gas, que aprovecha el exceso de electricidad generada por el viento, que no se puede almacenar, para obtener hidrógeno y, con él, metano, el cual se quiere aprovechar como combustible para el coche y la calefacción. Utiliza los excedentes de energía eólica y genera menos CO_2 que las fuentes de energía no renovables.

El CO_2 que emite el gas metano es inferior al de la gasolina y el gasóleo de calefacción.

5.6. Nuovi sistemi

Si sviluppano costantemente strategie che sfruttano le risorse naturali. La Audi, ad esempio, sta per mettere in pratica il progetto e-gas, in cui si sfrutta l'eccesso di elettricità generata dal vento, che non è possibile immagazzinare, per ottenere idrogeno e, con ciò, metano. S'intende sfruttare questo gas come combustibile per le automobili ed il riscaldamento. Non è al 100% esente da emissioni, però utilizza gli eccedenti d'energia eolica e genera meno CO_2 rispetto alle fonti d'energia non rinnovabili.

Il CO_2 che emette il gas metano è inferiore a quello della benzina e il gasolio del riscaldamento.

5.6. Novos sistemas

Estão em constante desenvolvimento estratégias que aproveitam os recursos naturais. A Audi, por exemplo, está a ponto de pôr em prática o projecto e-gas, no qual se aproveita o excesso de electricidade gerada pelo vento, que não se pode armazenar, para obter hidrogénio e, com este, metano. Pretende-se aproveitar este gás como combustível para o carro e para o aquecimento. Não é 100% livre de emissões, mas utiliza os excedentes de energia eólica e gera menos CO_2 que as fontes de energia não renováveis.

O CO_2 emitido pelo gás metano é inferior ao da gasolina e do gasóleo de aquecimento.

6. SAVING WATER

6. WASSEREINSPARUNG

6. ÉCONOMIE D'EAU

6. WATERBESPARING

6. AHORRO DE AGUA

6. RISPARMIO IDRICO

6. POUPANÇA DE ÁGUA

*6.1

6.1. Rainwater collection and harvesting systems

Rainwater exploitation systems use rainwater to be re-used in gardens, dishwashers and washing machines. The capacity of the cisterns is decided on depending on rainfall and the needs of each household. Cisterns must be protected from dirt, light and excessive heat and it is recommended that they be situated underground and filters and purifying systems be installed.

The cisterns must be made with materials able to withstand corrosion and biological agents. Galvanised steel is a good choice for outdoor tanks.

6.1. Aufnahme- und Auffangsysteme für Regenwasser

Die Regenwassernutzungssysteme fangen das Regenwasser auf, um es in Gärten, Geschirrspülern oder Waschmaschinen wiederzuverwenden. Das Fassungsvermögen der Tanks wird entsprechend der Regenfallmengen und der Bedarfe der einzelnen Wohnhäuser bestimmt. Die Tanks müssen abgedeckt sein, um Verschmutzungen, Licht oder übermäßige Wärme zu vermeiden. Aus diesem Grund wird empfohlen, sie unterirdisch zu installieren und Filter und Reinigungssysteme einzubauen.

Die Tankmaterialien müssen rostfest und gegen biologische Auswirkungen beständig sein. Edelstahl ist eine gute Option für Außentanks.

6.1. Systèmes de captation et collecte des eaux pluviales

Les circuits de récupération des eaux pluviales sont prévus pour que l'eau soit utilisée dans les jardins, lave-vaisselles ou lave-linges. La contenance des réservoirs se calcule en fonction de la pluviométrie et des besoins de chaque maison. Les réserves d'eau doivent être protégées de toute pollution, de la lumière et d'une chaleur excessive. Il est donc conseillé de les enterrer à faible profondeur et d'installer des filtres et un système de purification.

Les cuves ou citernes doivent être réalisées dans des matériaux résistants à la corrosion et aux agents biologiques. L'acier galvanisé convient très bien pour les réservoirs en extérieur.

6.1. Regenwateropvangsystemen
Regenwatersystemen vangen regenwater op om dit opnieuw te gebruiken voor tuinen, vaatwassers of wasmachines. De capaciteit van de tanks wordt bepaald op grond van de gemeten regenval en van de behoeften de woning. De waterreservoirs kunnen beschermd worden om vuil, licht of te veel warmte te vermijden. Vandaar dat wordt aanbevolen om de tanks onder de grond te installeren en filters en zuiveringssystemen aan te brengen.

Het voor de reservoirs gebruikte materiaal moet bestand zijn tegen corrosie en tegen biologische agentia. Gegalvaniseerd staal is een goede keuze voor buitentanks.

6.1. Sistemas de captación y recolección de aguas pluviales
Los sistemas de aprovechamiento de las aguas pluviales recuperan el agua de la lluvia para reutilizarla en jardines, lavavajillas o lavadoras. La capacidad de los depósitos se decide en función de la pluviometría y de las necesidades de cada residencia. Los depósitos deben estar protegidos para evitar la suciedad, la luz o el exceso de calor, por lo que se recomienda enterrarlos bajo tierra e instalar filtros y sistemas de depuración.

Los materiales de los depósitos deben ser resistentes a la corrosión y a los agentes biológicos. El acero galvanizado es una buena opción para tanques exteriores.

6.1. Sistema di captazione e raccolta di acque piovane
I sistemi di sfruttamento delle acque piovane recuperano l'acqua della pioggia per riutilizzarla in giardini, lavastoviglie o lavatrici. La capacità dei depositi si decide in funzione della pluviometria e delle necessità di ogni abitazione. I depositi devono essere protetti per evitare la sporcizia, la luce o l'eccesso di calore, ragion per cui se ne consiglia l'interramento e l'installazione di filtri e sistemi di depurazione.

I materiali dei serbatoi devono essere resistenti alla corrosione ed agli agenti biologici. L'acciaio galvanizzato è una buona opzione per serbatoi esterni.

6.1. Sistemas de captação e recolha de águas pluviais
Os sistemas de aproveitamento das águas pluviais recuperam a água da chuva para a reutilizar em jardins, máquinas de lavar louça ou roupa. A capacidade dos depósitos é definida em função da pluviosidade e das necessidades de cada residência. Os depósitos devem estar protegidos para evitar a sujidade, a luz ou o excesso de calor, pelo que é recomendável enterrá-los debaixo de terra e instalar filtros e sistemas de depuração.

Os materiais dos depósitos devem ser resistentes à corrosão e aos agentes biológicos. O aço galvanizado é uma boa opção para tanques exteriores.

6.2. Re-using greywater
Greywater is that generated by washing machines, showers and bathtubs. It is different from sewage or blackwater because it contains no *Escherichia coli* bacteria. The purification of the water, with a biological filtration system, allows it to be reused for watering gardens or for toilets. By not using drinking water, a substantial saving is made. This system needs a different pipe set-up in the house but the economical and environmental saving outweigh this.

The grey lines of the chart show the sewage; the blue lines show the greywater which will be stored and the red lines show how the water is reused.

6.2. Brauchwasserwiederverwendung
Brauchwasser entsteht in Waschmaschinen, Duschen und Badewannen. Es unterscheidet sich vom Schmutzwasser, da es keine *Escherichia coli* Bakterien enthält. Die Klärung dieses Wasser durch Absetzung oder biologische Filter ermöglicht dessen Wiederverwendung zur Gartenbewässerung oder in WCs. Indem hierfür kein Trinkwasser eingesetzt wird, entsteht eine hohe Einsparung. Bei diesem System ist zwar eine zusätzliche Kanalisierung zur Hauskanalisierung erforderlich, aber die wirtschaftliche Einsparung und der Umweltschutz rechtfertigen die Maßnahme.

Die grauen Linien auf der Zeichnung zeigen das Schmutzwasser, die blauen das Brauchwasser, das in einen Tank geführt wird. Mit den roten Linien wird gezeigt, wofür das Wasser wiederverwendet wird.

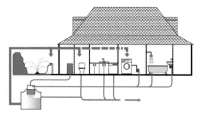

© Guillermo Pfaff. Source: Tanked Australia   * 6.2

6.2. Réutilisation des eaux grises

Les eaux grises sont celles qui proviennent des machines à laver, des douches et des baignoires. Elles sont différentes des eaux noires (WC) parce qu'elles ne contiennent pas la bactérie *Escherichia coli*. Le traitement de ces eaux, par décantation ou filtrages biologiques, les rend utilisables pour l'arrosage des jardins ou pour les chasses d'eau. On réalise ainsi des économies importantes d'eau potable. Le réemploi des eaux grises demande la pose d'une tuyauterie autonome dans le logement et donc un investissement supplémentaire, mais il est vite récupéré par les économies sur les factures et par la satisfaction d'avoir fait un choix écologique.

Les lignes grises du graphique représentent les eaux noires ; les bleues, les eaux grises qui vont être stockées tandis que les lignes rouges indiquent leur utilisation.

6.2. Hergebruik van grijs water

Grijs water is water afkomstig van wasmachines, douches en badkuipen. Het verschilt van riool- of zwart water omdat het geen *Escherichia coli* bacteriën bevat. Door de zuivering van het water, d.m.v. decanteren of biologische filters, kan dit water hergebruikt worden voor het sproeien van tuinen of voor wc's. Door geen drinkwater te verbruiken wordt veel water bespaart. Dit systeem vergt een ander buizennet in de woning, maar de geld- en milieubesparing maakt de balans op.

De grijze lijnen van de grafiek vertegenwoordigen het zwarte water; de blauwe het grijze water dat in een reservoir terechtkomt en de rode lijnen geven aan waarvoor het water wordt hergebruikt.

6.2. Reutilización de aguas grises

Las aguas grises son las generadas por lavadoras, duchas y bañeras. Se distinguen de las cloacales o negras porque no contienen bacterias *Escherichia coli*. La depuración del agua, con el decantado o los filtros biológicos, permiten reutilizar este agua para riego de jardines o para retretes. Al no consumirse agua potable, se realiza un gran ahorro. Este sistema requiere una canalización diferente en la vivienda, pero el ahorro económico y medioambiental decantan la balanza.

Las líneas grises del gráfico muestran las aguas negras; las azules las aguas grises que van a parar a un depósito y las líneas rojas muestran en qué se reutiliza el agua.

6.2. Riutilizzo delle acque grigie

Le acque grigie sono quelle generate dalle lavatrici, dalle docce e dalle vasche da bagno. Si differenziano da quelle cloacali, o nere, perché sono prive di batteri *Escherichia coli*. La depurazione dell'acqua con la decantazione o i filtri biologici, permette di riutilizzarle per l'irrigazione di giardini o per i WC. Evitare il consumo di acqua potabile consente un notevole risparmio. Questo sistema richiede una canalizzazione diversa nell'abitazione, però il consumo economico e ambientale fanno decantare la bilancia a favore di questo sistema.

Le linee grigie del grafico mostrano le acque nere; quelle blu le acque grigie che vanno a parare in un deposito, mentre le linee rosse mostrano in che modo viene riutilizzata l'acqua.

6.2. Reutilização de águas cinzentas

As águas cinzentas são as geradas por máquinas de lavar roupa, duches e banheiras. Diferenciam-se das cloacais ou negras porque não contêm bactérias *Escherichia coli*. A depuração da água, com a decantação ou com os filtros biológicos, permite reutilizar esta água na rega de jardins ou nas sanitas. Ao não se consumir água potável, realiza-se uma grande poupança. Este sistema requer uma canalização diferente na habitação, mas a poupança económica e o ganho ambiental fazem pender a balança.

As linhas cinzentas do gráfico mostram as águas negras; as azuis, as águas cinzentas que vão parar a um depósito e as linhas vermelhas mostram em que se reutiliza a água.

6.3. Water saving systems

One of the first water saving measures consists in checking there are no leaks in the installation. Others are habits changes such as showering instead of taking baths or systems which allow saving water with flow regulators or dual flush toilets. More efficient, class A, electrical appliances which use less water, should be purchased. Drip irrigation systems are recommended for gardens as is the planting of native plants adapted to the local rainfall.

Drip irrigation systems save anywhere between 40 and 60% water in comparison with traditional systems.

6.3. Wassereinsparungssysteme

Eine der ersten Maßnahmen zur Wassereinsparung besteht darin, zu prüfen, ob Lecks in der Installation vorhanden sind. Eine weitere Maßnahme stellen die Gewohnheiten wie Duschen statt Baden oder die Systeme

*6.3

zur Wassereinsparung wie Durchflussregler oder WC-Behälter mit Doppelentladung dar. Es sollen Hausgeräte mit höherer Energieeffizienz, d. h. A-Klasse, angeschafft werden, da sie weniger Wasser benötigen. In den Gärten wird empfohlen, Tropfenberieselung einzubauen und bodenständige Vegetation, die an die lokalen Regenwassermengen gewöhnt ist, anzupflanzen.

Mit der Tropfenberieselung erzielt man zwischen 40 und 60 % Wassereinsparung im Vergleich zu herkömmlichen Systemen.

6.3. Pour économiser l'eau

Une des premières mesures à prendre est de vérifier qu'il n'y a pas de fuite dans la tuyauterie. Ensuite, il faut changer ses habitudes, renoncer au bain et préférer la douche, poser des réducteurs de pression sur la robinetterie et choisir des chasses d'eau à double commande. Les appareils électroménagers en classe A pour l'efficacité énergétique consomment également moins d'eau. Dans les jardins, il est recommandé d'installer un arrosage goutte à goutte et de planter une végétation endémique qui se contente de la pluviométrie locale.

L'arrosage goutte à goutte permet de réaliser une économie se situant entre 40 et 60 % par rapport à l'arrosage traditionnel.

6.3. Waterbesparingssystemen

Een van de eerste maatregelen om water te besparen bestaat uit het controleren van de installatie op lekken. Andere maatregelen zijn gewoonten zoals het douchen in plaats van een bad nemen of systemen waarmee water kan worden bespaard zoals debietregelaars of stortbakken met dubbele spoeling (spaarknop). Er moeten klasse A huishoudelijke apparaten met een hogere energie-efficiëntie, die minder water gebruiken, worden gekocht. In tuinen wordt aanbevolen om een druppelirrigatiesysteem te installeren en bij de plaatselijke regenval passende autochtone plantensoorten te planten.

Met druppelirrigatie kan in vergelijking met traditionele systemen tussen 40 en 60% water worden bespaard.

6.3. Sistemas de ahorro de agua

Una de las primeras medidas para el ahorro de agua consiste en revisar que no existan fugas en la instalación. También es recomendable adoptar buenos hábitos, como tomar duchas en vez de baños, instalar sistemas que permiten ahorrar agua, como los reguladores de caudal o las cisternas de doble descarga, y adquirir electrodomésticos de clase A, de mayor eficiencia energética, que utilizan menos agua. En los jardines se recomienda instalar riego por goteo y plantar vegetación autóctona adaptada a la pluviometría local.

El riego por goteo permite un ahorro de agua de entre un 40 y un 60% respecto a los sistemas tradicionales.

6.3. Sistema di risparmio idrico

Una delle prime misure per il risparmio idrico consiste nel controllare le installazioni per accertarsi che non esistono fughe. Altre misure sono rappresentate dall'implementazione di buone prassi come farsi docce anziché bagni o ricorrere a sistemi che consentono il risparmio idrico come i regolatori di portata o WC a doppia scarica. Si devono acquistare elettrodomestici di maggiore efficienza energetica, di classe A, che utilizzino una minore quantità d'acqua. Nei giardini si consiglia d'installare impianti d'irrigazione a goccia e di piantare vegetazione autoctona adatta alla pluviometria locale.

Gli impianti d'irrigazione a goccia permettono un risparmio idrico del 40 / 60% circa rispetto ai sistemi tradizionali.

6.3. Sistemas de poupança de água

Uma das primeiras medidas para a poupança de água consiste em verificar se não existem fugas na instalação. Outras são hábitos, tais como tomar duche em vez de banho de imersão, ou sistemas que permitem poupar água, tais como os reguladores de caudal ou os autoclismos de dupla descarga. Devem comprar-se electrodomésticos de maior eficiência energética, de classe A, que utilizam menos água. Nos jardins é recomendável instalar rega gota a gota e plantar vegetação autóctone adaptada à pluviosidade local.

A rega gota a gota permite uma poupança de água entre cerca de 40 e 60% em relação aos sistemas tradicionais.

EDGE HOUSE

Studio B Architects
Aspen, CO, USA
© Derek Skalko, Raul J. Garcia, Aspen Architectural Photography

This home is located on a slope integrated into the land. The eaves protect from the sun and the solar panels heat the pool water. The natural materials indoors, such as bamboo, are an example of an architecture that combines comfort with sustainability, supplemented by water-saving devices and lighting that reduces energy costs.

Dieses Wohnhaus wurde am Berghang errichtet, wo es sich in die natürliche Umgebung einfügt. Die Vordächer schützen vor der Sonneneinstrahlung, das Wasser im Swimmingpool wird durch die Solarpaneele erwärmt. Die im Innenbereich verwendeten Naturmaterialien wie Bambus stehen für eine Bauweise, die Komfort und Nachhaltigkeit verbindet. Zusätzlich wurden Maßnahmen zur Reduzierung des Wasserverbrauchs und zur Verbesserung der natürlichen Ausleuchtung getroffen, um den Energieverbrauch zu senken.

Cette résidence suit la pente pour s'intégrer au terrain. Les auvents protègent du soleil et les panneaux solaires chauffent l'eau de la piscine. Les matériaux naturels employés à l'intérieur, comme le bambou, reflètent les préoccupations d'une architecture soucieuse d'offrir le confort dans le respect de l'environnement comme en témoignent les installations prévues pour économiser l'eau et réduire le coût en énergie de l'éclairage.

Deze woning is gelegen op een helling, zodat hij in het landschap geïntegreerd is. De luifeldaken beschermen tegen de zon en het zwembadwater wordt verwarmd door zonnepanelen. De natuurlijke materialen in het interieur, zoals bamboe, weerspiegelen een architectuur die comfort met duurzaamheid combineert, aangevuld met mechanismen voor waterbesparing en verlichting, waardoor het energieverbruik omlaag wordt gebracht.

Esta residencia está situada en la pendiente para integrarse en el terreno. Los aleros protegen del sol y las placas solares calientan el agua de la piscina. Los materiales naturales del interior, como el bambú, reflejan una arquitectura que une confort con sostenibilidad, complementada por mecanismos de ahorro de agua e iluminación que reducen el gasto energético.

Questa abitazione si trova su un terreno in pendenza integrandosi con questo. Il cornicione protegge dal sole e i pannelli solari riscaldano l'acqua della piscina. I materiali naturali che troviamo all'interno, come il bambù, riflettono un'architettura che unisce comfort e sostenibilità, integrata da meccanismi di risparmio idrico e di illuminazione che riducono le spese energetiche.

Esta habitação está situada num declive de forma a integrar-se no terreno. Os beirais protegem do sol e os painéis solares aquecem a água da piscina. Os materiais naturais do interior, como o bambu, reflectem uma arquitetura que combina conforto com sustentabilidade, complementada por mecanismos de poupança de água e iluminação que reduzem o consumo energético.

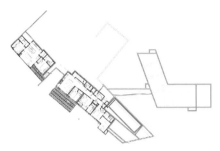

Lower level / Étage inférieur

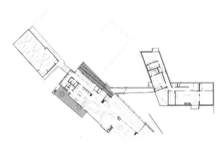

Main level / Étage principal

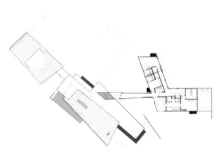

Upper level / Étage supérieur

HOUSE FOR TWO ARTISTS

Marcy Wong Donn Logan Architects
Sonoma County, CA, USA
© Mark Citret

The most remarkable aspect of this construction is the use of trees from the estate. The choice of the trees to be felled followed the practice of selection cutting, increasing the resistance of the forest in case of fire. In addition, the use of natural resources reduces CO_2 emissions that the transportation and manufacturing of the materials involves.

Besonders hervorzuheben ist die Tatsache, dass für dieses Bauprojekt Bäume des Grundstücks verwendet wurden. Die Auswahl der zu fällenden Bäume erfolgte im Sinne einer selektiven Säuberung des Baugrunds, um die Widerstandskraft des Waldes bei einem Brand zu erhöhen. Die Nutzung natürlicher Ressourcen reduzierte außerdem den CO_2-Ausstoß durch Transport und Fertigung der Baumaterialien.

L'aspect le plus remarquable de cette construction est l'utilisation des arbres de la propriété, ce qui a permis, en même temps, de nettoyer la parcelle tout en favorisant la résistance de la forêt aux incendies. L'utilisation des ressources naturelles, on le sait, réduit les rejets de CO_2 inhérents au transport et à la fabrication des matériaux.

Het opvallendste aspect van deze bouw is het gebruik van de bomen op het terrein. De beslissing omtrent welke bomen moesten worden omgezaagd beantwoordde aan een selectieve houtkap op het perceel, waardoor de resistentie van het bos in geval van brand zou worden vergroot. Bovendien is dankzij optimaal gebruik van de natuurlijke hulpbronnen de CO_2-uitstoot, als gevolg van vervoer en de vervaardiging van materialen, gereduceerd.

El aspecto más destacable de esta construcción es el uso de los árboles de la propiedad. La elección de los que debían talarse obedeció a una limpieza selectiva de la parcela, que aumentaría la resistencia del bosque en caso de incendio. Además, el aprovechamiento de los recursos naturales reduce la emisión de CO_2 derivados del transporte y la fabricación de materiales.

L'aspetto più peculiare di questa costruzione è l'uso degli alberi presenti sul terreno della proprietà. La scelta di quelli da abbattere è stata dettata da una pulizia selettiva del terreno, aumentando la resistenza del bosco in caso di incendio. Inoltre, l'utilizzo di risorse naturali riduce le emissioni di CO_2 causate dal trasporto e dalla produzione dei materiali.

O aspecto de maior destaque nesta construção é o uso das árvores da propriedade. A escolha das árvores que deveriam ser derrubadas obedeceu a um critério de limpeza selectiva da parcela, com vista a aumentar a resistência da floresta em caso de incêndio. Além disso, o aproveitamento dos recursos naturais reduz a emissão de CO_2 implicada no transporte e no fabrico de materiais.

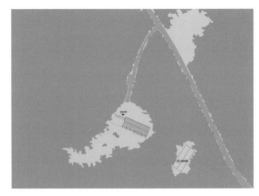

Location plan / Plan de situation

Elevations / Élévations

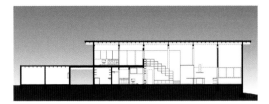

Section / Vue en coupe

1. Storage / Rangements
2. Bathroom / Salle de bains
3. Laundry / Buanderie
4. Living room / Salon
5. Dining room / Salle à manger
6. Kitchen / Cuisine
7. Study / Bureau
8. Bedroom / Chambre
9. Roof / Toiture
10. Arcade / Arcade
11. Terrace / Terrasse
12. Porch / Porche

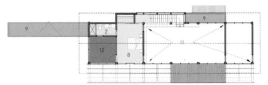

Floor plans / Étages

KOBY COTTAGE

Garrison Architects
Albion, MI, USA
© Garrison Architects

This modular prefabricated house consists of two volumes separated to improve lighting and ensure privacy. The KFS structural steel tubular system, which allows the construction of multi-storey buildings up to 12 floors, reduces CO_2 emissions and the construction time. The rest of the materials ensure optimum insulation.

Dieses modulare Fertighaus besteht aus zwei Baukörpern, die voneinander getrennt sind, um die Ausleuchtung zu verbessern und für ausreichend Privatsphäre zu sorgen. Dank der Rohrstruktur aus KFS-Stahl, die eine serienmäßige Herstellung von bis zu 12 Etagen ermöglicht, können die CO_2-Emissionen und die Bauzeit gesenkt werden. Die übrigen verwendeten Materialien gewährleisten eine optimale Isolierung.

Les deux volumes distincts qui composent cet immeuble modulaire préfabriqué favorisent l'entrée de la lumière et protègent l'intimité de ses habitants. La structure tubulaire en acier KFS, qui permet de construire jusqu'à 12 appartements en série, réduit les émissions de CO_2 et la durée de construction. Les autres matériaux assurent une isolation optimale.

Dit geprefabriceerde modulaire huis heeft twee volumen die van elkaar gescheiden zijn voor een betere lichtinval en om privacy te garanderen. Het systeem van een buisvormige structuur van KFS-staal, waarmee seriebouw kan worden gemaakt tot 12 flats, verminderd de CO_2-uitstoot en de bouwtijd. De overige materialen garanderen een optimale isolatie.

Esta casa modular prefabricada consta de dos volúmenes separados para mejorar la iluminación y asegurar la privacidad. El sistema de estructura tubular de acero KFS, que permite construcciones en serie de hasta 12 pisos, reduce las emisiones de CO_2 y el tiempo de construcción. El resto de los materiales aseguran un óptimo aislamiento.

Questa casa modulare prefabbricata comprende due volumi separati per migliorare l'illuminazione e garantire la privacy. Il sistema con una struttura tubolare in acciaio KFS, che consente di realizzare edifici in serie fino a 12 piani, riduce le emissioni di CO_2 e i tempi di costruzione. Gli altri materiali impiegati garantiscono un isolamento ottimale.

Esta casa modular pré-fabricada é composta por dois volumes separados para melhorar a iluminação e assegurar a privacidade. O sistema de estrutura tubular de aço KFS, que permite construções em série até 12 pisos, reduz as emissões de CO_2 e o tempo de construção. Os restantes materiais asseguram um óptimo isolamento.

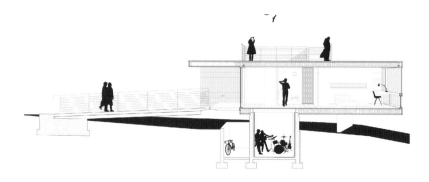

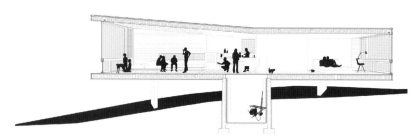

Sections / Vue en coupe

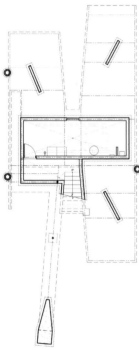

Basement floor / Sous-sol

Ground floor / Rez-de-chaussée

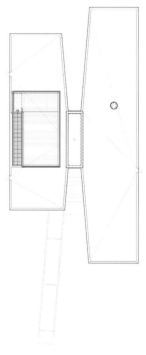

Roof floor / Niveau de la toiture

TUCSON MOUNTAIN RETREAT

Dust Design Build
Tucson, AZ, USA
© Tim Fuller, Cade Hayes

This home under construction in the Arizona desert includes several sustainable strategies: the use of local materials, such as earth, minimizing the environmental impact, the orientation and the windows create cross ventilation, and a few rainwater tanks and future solar panels will supply the home with water and energy.

Bei diesem Haus, das in der Wüste von Arizona gebaut wird, werden mehrere Nachhaltigkeitsstrategien umgesetzt: Die Verwendung lokaler Baumaterialien wie Lehm minimiert die Umweltbelastung, Ausrichtung und Fenster ermöglichen eine Kreuzlüftung, mehrere Regenwassertanks sowie später installierte Sonnenkollektoren versorgen das Haus mit Wasser und Strom.

Cette villa en construction dans le désert d'Arizona associe plusieurs stratégies de développement durable. L'usage de matériaux locaux comme la terre minimise son impact sur l'environnement. L'orientation et l'emplacement des fenêtres créent une ventilation croisée. Par la suite, les réservoirs d'eaux pluviales et les panneaux solaires fourniront eau et énergie au logement.

Bij deze woning in aanbouw, gelegen in de woestijn van Arizona, zijn diverse duurzame strategieën gebruikt: het gebruik van plaatselijke materialen zoals grond, vermindert de impact op het milieu; de oriëntatie en de ramen zorgen voor gekruiste ventilatie en de regentonnen en enkele zonnepanelen die in de toekomst zullen worden geïnstalleerd voorzien in de water- en energiebehoeften van de woning.

Esta residencia en construcción del desierto de Arizona incluye varias estrategias sostenibles: el uso de materiales locales, como la tierra, minimiza el impacto ambiental; la orientación y las ventanas crean ventilación cruzada, y unos tanques de aguas pluviales y unas futuras placas solares abastecen de agua y energía a la vivienda.

Questa casa in costruzione nel deserto dell'Arizona prevede l'applicazione di varie strategie di sostenibilità: l'uso di materiali locali come la terra riduce al minimo l'impatto ambientale; l'orientamento e le finestre creano ventilazione incrociata; dei serbatoi di raccolta dell'acqua piovana e la futura applicazione di pannelli solari garantiscono il necessario approvvigionamento idrico ed energetico della struttura.

Esta casa em construção no deserto do Arizona inclui várias estratégias sustentáveis: o uso de materiais locais, como a terra, minimiza o impacto ambiental; a orientação e as janelas criam ventilação cruzada. Tanques de águas pluviais e painéis solares a instalar no futuro irão abastecer a habitação de água e energia.

Location plan / Plan de situation

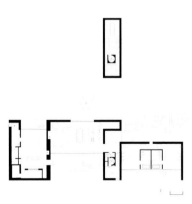

Floor plan / Étage

WRAP HOUSE

Studio B Architects
Aspen, CO, USA
© Derek Skalko, Raul J. Garcia

This home incorporates elements that encourage sustainability. The design achieves good cross ventilation and the eaves only allow the entry of winter sun. Natural materials and recycled wood were used. The faucets, lighting, radiant heating and low-e windows improve the energy efficiency of the home.

Dieses Haus weist zahlreiche Elemente für mehr Nachhaltigkeit auf. Durch das besondere Design wird die Kreuzlüftung ermöglicht und die Vordächer lassen das Sonnenlicht nur im Winter direkt einfallen. Armaturen, Beleuchtung, Fußbodenheizung und Low-E-Fenster steigern die Energieeffizienz des Gebäudes.

Cette maison intègre plusieurs éléments favorables au développement durable. Le plan offre une bonne ventilation croisée et les auvents laissent le soleil entrer uniquement en hiver. On a utilisé des matériaux naturels et des bois recyclés. La robinetterie, l'éclairage, le chauffage radiant et les vitrages à basse émissivité améliorent encore l'efficacité énergétique de la construction.

Dit huis heeft elementen die bijdragen aan duurzaamheid. Het ontwerp voorziet in een goede kruisventilatie en dankzij de overstekende dakranden schijnt het zonlicht alleen in de winter naar binnen. Er is gebruik gemaakt van natuurlijke en gerecyclede materialen. De kranen, verlichting, stralingsverwarming en de *low-e* glazen verbeteren de energie-efficiënte van de woning.

Esta casa incorpora elementos que ayudan a la sostenibilidad. El diseño consigue una buena ventilación cruzada y los aleros permiten la entrada del sol solamente en invierno. Se utilizaron materiales naturales y madera reciclada. La grifería, la iluminación, la calefacción radiante y los cristales Low-e mejoran la eficiencia energética de la residencia.

Questa casa utilizza elementi che contribuiscono alla sostenibilità. Il progetto garantisce una buona ventilazione incrociata e le protezioni consentono l'ingresso della luce solare solo in inverno. Sono stati impiegati materiali naturali e legno riciclato. La rubinetteria, l'illuminazione, il riscaldamento radiante e i vetri *low-e* (a basso emissivo) migliorano l'efficienza energetica dell'abitazione.

Esta casa incorpora elementos que contribuem para a sustentabilidade. O design assegura uma boa ventilação cruzada e os beirais permitem a entrada do sol somente no Inverno. Foram utilizados materiais naturais e madeira reciclada. A canalização, a iluminação, o aquecimento radiante e os vidros *low-e* melhoram a eficiência energética da habitação.

Ground floor / Rez-de-chaussée

Second floor / Premier étage

Third floor / Deuxième étage

Roof floor / Terrasse couverte

POTRERO HOUSE

Cary Bernstein Architect
San Francisco, CA, USA
© Cesar Rubio

The objectives of the extension were to build vertically to preserve the garden and do so sustainably. The reform achieved a reduction of energy consumption, as well as better lighting and ventilation. Other features of the house are radiant heating, certified timber and a structure prepared for the installation of solar panels.

Bei diesem Ausbau sollte nachhaltig in die Höhe gebaut werden, um den Garten zu erhalten. Durch den Umbau konnte der Energieverbrauch gesenkt und die Ausleuchtung und Belüftung konnten verbessert werden. Zu den weiteren Merkmalen dieses Hauses gehören eine Fußbodenheizung, die Verwendung zertifizierter Hölzer und eine Struktur, die für die spätere Installation von Sonnenkollektoren geeignet ist.

Il s'agissait d'agrandir la maison tout en préservant le jardin et en adoptant une démarche de développement durable. C'est la raison pour laquelle l'extension s'est faite verticalement. La rénovation a permis une réduction de la consommation d'énergie, tout en améliorant l'éclairage et la ventilation. Les autres caractéristiques de la maison sont le chauffage radiant, le bois labellisé et une structure prête à recevoir des panneaux solaires.

De doelstellingen voor de uitbouw waren om verticaal te bouwen, om de tuin te behouden, en om dat op duurzame wijze te doen. De verbouwing bracht bovendien een lager energieverbruik met zich mede, alsmede een verbeterde verlichting en ventilatie. Andere kenmerken van het huis zijn stralingsverwarming, gecertificeerd hout en een structuur die geschikt is om zonnepanelen te installeren.

Los objetivos de la ampliación eran construir verticalmente para conservar el jardín y hacerlo de forma sostenible. La reforma consiguió una reducción del consumo energético, así como una mejor iluminación y ventilación. Otras de las características de la casa son la calefacción radiante, la madera certificada y una estructura preparada para instalar placas solares.

Lo scopo di questo ampliamento era costruire in verticale per preservare il giardino e fare tutto questo in modo sostenibile. La ristrutturazione ha consentito di ridurre i consumi energetici, oltre a ottenere una migliore illuminazione e ventilazione. Altre caratteristiche della casa sono il riscaldamento radiante, l'uso di legname certificato e una struttura predisposta per l'installazione di pannelli solari.

Os objectivos da ampliação eram construir verticalmente para conservar o jardim e fazê-lo de forma sustentável. A reforma conseguiu uma redução do consumo energético, bem como uma melhor iluminação e ventilação. Outras das características da casa são o aquecimento radiante, a madeira certificada e uma estrutura preparada para a instalação de painéis solares.

Rendering / Représentation en 3D

Location plan / Plan de situation

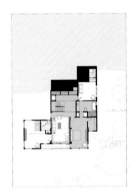

Basement floor / Sous-sol

Ground floor / Rez-de-chaussée

Second floor / Premier étage

MONTECITO RESIDENCE

Barton Myers Associates
Montecito, CA, USA
© Ciro Coelho/CiroCoelho.com

The modular construction of this house is one way to reduce the environmental impact. Everything that contributes to reducing the construction time will benefit the ecosystems and decrease CO_2 emissions. And if the majority of metal is recycled and the orientation of the house is according to sustainable criteria, the ecological footprint is reduced.

Der modulare Aufbau dieses Wohnhauses stellt eine ausgezeichnete Art und Weise zur Minderung der Umweltbelastung dar. Alle Maßnahmen, die zu einer Verkürzung der Bauzeit führen, haben Vorteile für die bestehenden Ökosysteme und eine Verringerung des CO_2-Ausstoßes zur Folge. Auch die Verwendung eines möglichst großen Anteils von recyceltem Metall und die Ausrichtung des Hauses unter Berücksichtigung der Nachhaltigkeitskriterien tragen zu einer Reduzierung des ökologischen Fußabdrucks bei.

La construction modulaire est l'une des manières de diminuer l'impact d'une construction sur l'environnement. Tout ce qui participe à réduire la durée du chantier se traduit par un gain pour les écosystèmes et une baisse des émissions de CO_2. En recyclant la majeure partie du métal et par une orientation judicieusement choisie selon des critères durables, son empreinte sur l'environnement se fait plus discret.

De modulaire bouw van dit huis is een manier om de impact op het milieu te verlagen. Alles wat erop gericht is om de bouwtijd te verkorten, komt tot uitdrukking in voordelen voor de ecosystemen en een vermindering van de CO_2-uitstoot. En als het merendeel van het metaal gerecycled is en het huis op grond van duurzame criteria is georiënteerd, is de ecologische voetafdruk kleiner.

La construcción modular de esta casa constituye una manera de reducir el impacto ambiental. Todo lo que sea acortar tiempo de edificación redunda en beneficio de los ecosistemas y en la disminución de las emisiones de CO_2. Y si la mayor parte del metal es reciclado y la orientación de la casa se hace con criterios sostenibles, se reduce la huella ambiental.

La struttura modulare di questa casa rappresenta un modo per ridurre l'impatto ambientale. Tutto ciò che contribuisce a ridurre i tempi di costruzione va a vantaggio degli ecosistemi e porta alla riduzione delle emissioni di CO_2. Se poi la maggior parte del metallo è riciclato e l'orientamento della casa segue criteri sostenibili, si riesce a ridurre l'impronta ambientale.

A construção modular desta casa constitui uma maneira de reduzir o impacto ambiental. Tudo o que implique redução no tempo de construção resulta em benefícios para os ecossistemas e na diminuição das emissões de CO_2. E se a maior parte do metal for reciclada e a orientação da casa for feita com critérios sustentáveis, a pegada ambiental será reduzida.

Sketch / Croquis

East elevation / Élévation est

North elevation / Élévation nord

West elevation / Élévation ouest

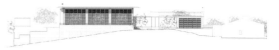

South elevation / Élévation sud

Floor plan / Étage

Site plan / Plan de situation

Sections / Vue en coupe

1. Terrace / Terrasse
2. Living – Dining / Salon – salle à manger
3. Kitchen / Cuisine
4. Reading / Coin lecture
5. Bar / Bar - Cave

6. Storage / Rangements
7. Pantry / Cellier
8. Powder room / Sanitaires
9. Mechanical room / Pièce technique
10. Library / Bibliothèque

11. Guest bath / Salle de bains de la chambre d'amis
12. Guest bedroom / Chambre d'amis
13. Master bath / Salle de bains principale
14. Closet / Débarras
15. Master bedroom / Chambre principale

16. Garden room / Appentis
17. Garage / Garage
18. Garden / Jardin
19. Firepit / Foyer ouvert
20. Fountain / Fontaine

GRID HOUSE

Forte, Gimenes & Marcondes Ferraz Arquitetos
Serra da Mantiqueira, Brazil
© Ale Shneider

All the aspects of the house are designed to reduce the ecological footprint. It has been erected on pillars to minimize the impact on the environment and local certified or recyclable materials have been used. The green roof, which thermally insulates the house and the local vegetation in the garden complete the bioclimatic proposals.

Sämtliche Aspekte dieses Hauses wurden durchdacht, um einen möglichst kleinen ökologische Fußabdruck zu erzielen. Der Bau steht auf Stelzen, um die Umweltbelastung zu minimieren, und es wurden lokale, zertifizierte oder recycelte Materialien verwendet. Das bepflanzte Dach, das als Wärmedämmung dient, und die Bepflanzung des Garten mit einheimischen Spezies runden die umgesetzten bioklimatischen Maßnahmen ab.

Tout a été pensé dans le but de réduire l'empreinte écologique de cette maison sur pilotis pour minimiser son impact sur l'environnement. Les matériaux employés sont locaux, labellisés ou recyclables. La toiture végétale, qui assure l'isolation thermique, et la végétation endémique du jardin complètent les dispositions prises pour en faire une habitation bioclimatique.

Alle aspecten van het huis zijn bedacht om de ecologische voetafdruk te verkleinen. Het is gebouwd op pilaren, om de impact op het milieu zo klein mogelijk te houden en er is gebruik gemaakt van plaatselijke, gecertificeerde of hergebruikbare materialen. Het plantendak, dat zorgt voor warmte-isolatie en de autochtone vegetatie van de tuin maken het geheel van bioklimatische maatregelen compleet.

Todos los aspectos de la casa están pensados para reducir la huella ecológica. Se ha ubicado sobre pilares para minimizar el impacto sobre el medio ambiente y se han utilizado materiales locales, certificados o reciclables. La cubierta vegetal, que aísla térmicamente, y la vegetación autóctona del jardín completan el conjunto de medidas bioclimáticas.

Tutti gli aspetti della casa sono pensati per ridurre l'impronta ecologica. La struttura poggia su pilastri per ridurre al minimo l'impatto sull'ambiente; sono inoltre stati utilizzati materiali locali, certificati o riciclabili. Il rivestimento vegetale che garantisce l'isolamento termico e la vegetazione autoctona del giardino completano l'insieme delle misure bioclimatiche.

Todos os aspectos da casa foram pensados com o intuito de reduzir a pegada ecológica. Foi colocada sobre pilares para minimizar o impacto sobre o ambiente e foram utilizados materiais locais, certificados ou recicláveis. A cobertura vegetal, que isola termicamente, e a vegetação autóctone do jardim completam o conjunto de medidas bioclimáticas.

Site plan / Plan de situation

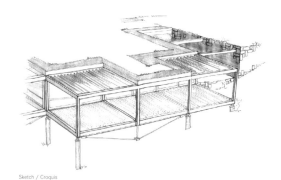

Sketch / Croquis

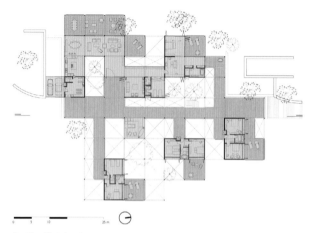

Ground floor / Rez-de-chaussée

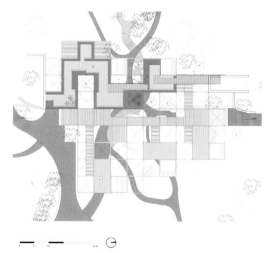

Roof plan / Terrasse couverte

CASA FAMILIA

Kevin deFreitas Architects
San Diego, CA, USA
© Harrison Photographic

This house was built to reduce the consumption of natural resources through passive and active strategies and the use of recyclable and sustainable materials. The home consumes 65% less electricity than a standard house and 55% less water than a similar sized house without sacrificing design and comfort.

Dieses Haus wurde mit dem Ziel entworfen, den Verbrauch natürlicher Ressourcen durch den Einsatz passiver und aktiver Strategien sowie durch die Verwendung recycelter und nachhaltiger Materialien zu reduzieren. Das Wohngebäude verbraucht 65 % weniger elektrische Energie als ein normales Haus und 55 % weniger Wasser als ein vergleichbar großer Bau, ohne dass bei Ästhetik und Komfort Abstriche gemacht werden mussten.

Cette villa a été pensée afin de minimiser sa consommation de ressources naturelles par l'association de stratégies passives et actives et l'empli de matériaux recyclés et durables. Elle consomme 65 % d'électricité de moins qu'une maison conventionnelle et 55 % d'eau de moins qu'un logement de surface comparable sans sacrifier ni l'esthétique ni le confort.

Dit huis is gebouwd met het doel het verbruik van natuurlijke hulpbronnen te verminderen dankzij passieve en actieve strategieën en het gebruik van recyclede en duurzame materialen. De woning verbruikt 65% minder elektriciteit dan een standaardhuis en 55% minder water dan een woning van vergelijkbare grootte, zonder dat dat ten koste gaat van esthetiek en comfort.

Esta casa se construyó con el objetivo de reducir el consumo de recursos naturales gracias a estrategias pasivas y activas y al uso de materiales reciclados y sostenibles. La residencia consume un 65% menos de electricidad que una casa estándar y un 55% menos de agua que una residencia de un tamaño comparable sin sacrificar la estética y el confort.

Questa casa è stata realizzata con l'obiettivo di ridurre il consumo delle risorse naturali attraverso strategie passive e attive e all'uso di materiali riciclati e sostenibili. L'edificio consuma il 65% in meno di elettricità di una casa normale e il 55% in meno di acqua rispetto a un'abitazione di dimensioni comparabili senza rinunciare a estetica e comfort.

Esta casa foi construída com o objectivo de reduzir o consumo de recursos naturais graças a estratégias passivas e activas e ao uso de materiais reciclados e sustentáveis. A habitação consome cerca de 65% menos electricidade que uma casa standard e cerca de 55% menos de água que uma casa com dimensões comparáveis sem sacrificar a estética e o conforto.

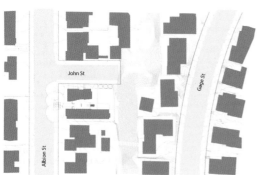

Site plan / Plan de situation

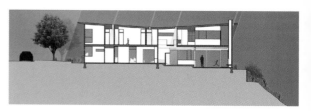

Section / Vue en coupe

Second floor – Ground floor / Premier étage – Rez-de-chaussée

1. Entrance / Entrée
2. Living room / Salon
3. Dining room / Salle à manger
4. Kitchen / Cuisine
5. Family room / Salle de séjour
6. Bedroom / Chambre
7. Dressing room / Dressing

8. Bathroom / Salle de bains
9. Outdoor dining / Salle à manger extérieure
10. Study / Bureau
11. Garage / Garage
12. Storage / Rangements
13. Playroom / Salle de loisirs
14. Laundry / Buanderie

15. Master bathroom / Salle de bains principale
16. Master bedroom / Chambre principale
17. Dressing room / Dressing
18. Terrace / Terrasse
19. Bridge / Pont

Green features diagram / Croquis des installations écologiques

1. Low-water native plant selection, artificial turf, drip irrigation / Végétation endémique, gazon artificiel, arrosage goutte à goutte
2. Reuse of windows from previously rehabilitated lofts, recycled carpet / Réemploi de fenêtres, moquette recyclée
3. Low environmental impact materials / Matériaux à faible impact sur l'environnement
4. Active methods: solar panels, radiant floor heating / Installations actives : panneaux solaires, chauffage radiant
5. Passive systems: naturally ventilated home, strategic use of natural daylighting / Installations passives : ventilation croisée, lumière du jour

ANGUILLA HOUSE

Paul Lukez Architecture
Sea Feathers Bay, Anguilla
© Paul Lukez

This home, located on a Caribbean Island, was built on rocky land. Given the climate and the orography, it was decided that the strategies should be passive: study the openings to create shade and collect the rainwater. In this way, the house is positioned over three cisterns and the location of the volumes protects from the northeast wind.

Dieses Wohnhaus auf einer Karibikinsel wurde auf felsigem Grund errichtet. Aufgrund des Klimas und der Orographie entschied man sich für passive Strategien, z. B. durchdachte Anordnung der Fassadenöffnungen für effektive Schatten und Auffangen des Regenwassers. Das Haus steht über drei Zisternen; die Lage der Baukörper schützt vor dem Nordostwind.

La demeure, située sur une île des Caraïbes, a été construite sur un terrain rocailleux. Compte tenu du climat et de l'orographie, les stratégies passives s'imposaient. L'emplacement des ouvertures a donc été étudié pour générer de l'ombre naturellement et un système de collecte des eaux de pluie a été mis en place. La maison repose sur trois citernes. L'implantation des volumes protège du vent du nord-est.

Deze woning, gelegen op een eiland in het Caraïbisch gebied, is op rotsachtige grond gebouwd. Gezien het klimaat en de orografie werd gekozen voor passieve strategieën: er is gekeken naar hoe er schaduw kon worden gecreëerd en naar de mogelijkheden om regenwater op te vangen. Onder het huis bevinden zich daarom drie regenputten en dankzij de ligging van de woongedeeltes wordt bescherming geboden tegen de noordoostenwind.

La residencia, situada en una isla del Caribe, se construyó sobre un terreno rocoso. Dados el clima y la orografía, se decidió que las estrategias serían pasivas: estudiar las aberturas para generar sombras y recolectar el agua de la lluvia. Así, la casa se asienta sobre tres cisternas y la situación de los volúmenes protege del viento del nordeste.

L'abitazione, situata su un'isola dei Caraibi, è stata edificata su un terreno roccioso. Considerando il clima e l'orografia, si è deciso di optare per strategie passive: studiare le aperture per generare ombre e raccogliere l'acqua piovana. La casa sovrasta tre cisterne e la distribuzione dei volumi protegge dal vento di nord-est.

A residência, situada numa ilha das Caraíbas, foi construída sobre um terreno rochoso. Considerando o clima e a orografia, decidiu-se que as estratégias seriam passivas: estudar as aberturas para criar sombras e recolher a água da chuva. Assim, a casa está assente sobre três cisternas e o posicionamento dos volumes protege-a do vento de nordeste.

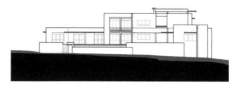

Elevations / Élévation

Sketches / Croquis

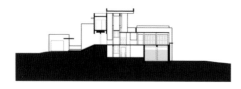

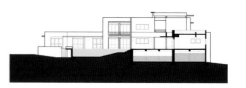

Sections / Vues en coupe

Foundation plan / Sous-sol – Rez-de-chaussée

First floor / Premier étage

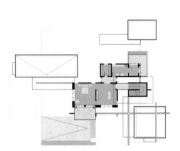

Second floor / Deuxième étage

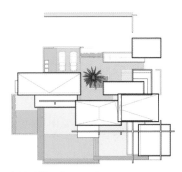

Roof plan / Toiture en terrasse couverte

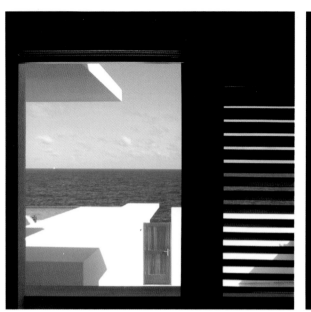

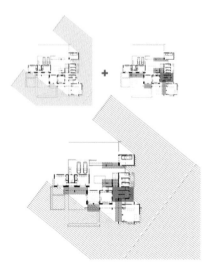

Wind and shades diagram / Diagramme des ombres et des vents

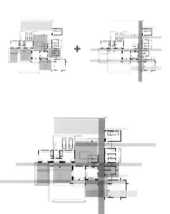

Spatial diagrams / Diagrammes dans l'espace

CASA TORCIDA

Eric Gartner, Coty Sidnam/SPG Architects
Osa Peninsula, Costa Rica
© Charles Lindsay

This magnificent home has been designed to be self-sufficient. The photovoltaic panels on the roof are complemented with a hydroelectric plant to provide energy. A rainwater collection system supplies the drinking water and graywater. The ventilation and shade systems combat the heat from the tropical climate.

Dieses beeindruckende Wohnhaus wurde als energieautarkes Gebäude entworfen. Die auf dem Dach installierten Photovoltaikpaneele zur Energieerzeugung werden durch ein kleines Wasserkraftwerk ergänzt. Ein Regenwasserauffangsystem versorgt das Haus mit Leitungs- und Grauwasser. Die Belüftung und die mit Bedacht designten Schattensysteme mildern die tropische Hitze.

Cette magnifique demeure a été conçue pour être autosuffisante. Une installation hydro-électrique complète les panneaux photovoltaïques de la toiture pour fournir l'énergie. Un système de collecte de l'eau de pluie fournit l'eau potable et les eaux grises. La ventilation et les ombres savamment créées combattent la chaleur du climat tropical.

Deze fantastische woning is ontworpen om zelfvoorzienend te zijn. De fotovoltaïsche panelen op het dak worden aangevuld met een hydro-elektrische installatie om energie te leveren. Een systeem voor het opvangen van regenwater levert drinkwater en grijs water. De ventilatie en de zonweringsystemen gaan de hitte van het tropische klimaat tegen.

Esta magnifica residencia se ha diseñado para que sea autosuficiente. Los paneles fotovoltaicos del tejado se complementan con una planta hidroeléctrica para proporcionar energía. Un sistema de recolección del agua de lluvia proporciona agua de boca y aguas grises. La ventilación y los sistemas de sombreado combaten el calor del clima tropical.

Questa magnifica struttura è stata progettata per essere autosufficiente. Ai pannelli fotovoltaici sul tetto si aggiunge un impianto idroelettrico per la produzione di energia. Un sistema per la raccolta dell'acqua piovana garantisce acqua potabile e viene usato per le acque grigie. La ventilazione e i sistemi di ombreggiamento combattono il calore che caratterizza il clima tropicale.

Esta casa magnifica foi concebida para ser auto-suficiente. Os painéis fotovoltaicos do telhado são complementados por uma unidade hidroelétrica para proporcionar energia. Um sistema de recolha da água da chuva proporciona água potável e águas cinzentas. A ventilação e os sistemas de sombra combatem o calor do clima tropical.

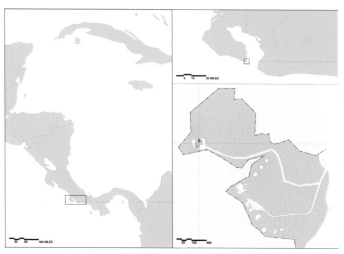

Site plan / Plans de situation

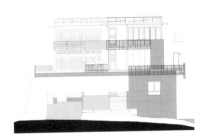

East elevation / Élévation est

Plan / Étage

IT HOUSE

Taalman Koch Architecture
Pioneertown, CA, USA
© Art Gray

The combination of prefabricated constructions, lightweight materials and passive and active energy-saving strategies convert this home into the perfect construction for isolated areas. The in situ assembly can be carried out by two people in a short period of time reducing the environmental impact on the land. Solar panels provide energy.

Die Kombination von vorgefertigten Elementen, leichten Baumaterialien sowie aktiven und passiven Strategien für mehr Energieersparnis macht dieses Haus zum perfekten Heim für abgeschiedene Standorte. Die Endmontage kann in kurzer Zeit von nur zwei Personen ausgeführt werden, wodurch die Belastung des Geländes reduziert wird. Sonnenkollektoren erzeugen elektrische Energie.

L'association de constructions préfabriquées, de matériaux légers et des stratégies actives et passives pour économiser l'énergie fait de cette maison une construction idéale pour les lieux isolés. Le montage in situ peut être réalisé par deux personnes en peu de temps, ce qui réduit l'impact sur l'environnement et le terrain. Les panneaux solaires fournissent l'énergie.

De combinatie van geprefabriceerde constructies, lichte materialen en actieve en passieve strategieën voor energiebesparing maken van dit huis de perfecte constructie voor afgelegen plaatsen. Het kan in korte tijd ter plekke in elkaar worden gezet door twee personen, waardoor de impact op de omgeving wordt verlaagd. De zonnepanelen zorgen voor de energie.

La combinación de estructuras prefabricadas, materiales ligeros y estrategias activas y pasivas de ahorro energético hacen de esta casa la construcción perfecta para lugares aislados. El montaje in situ pueden hacerlo dos personas en poco tiempo, con lo que se reduce el impacto ambiental en el terreno. Los paneles solares proporcionan energía.

La combinazione di strutture prefabbricate, materiali leggeri e strategie attive e passive di risparmio energetico rendono questa casa la scelta perfetta per i luoghi isolati. Il montaggio in loco può essere effettuato da due persone in poco tempo, riducendo l'impatto ambientale sul territorio. I pannelli solari forniscono energia.

A combinação de construções pré-fabricadas, materiais ligeiros e estratégias activas e passivas de poupança energética fazem desta casa a construção perfeita para locais isolados. A montagem no local podem ser efectuada por duas pessoas em pouco tempo, permitindo assim reduzir o impacto ambiental no terreno. Os painéis solares proporcionam energia.

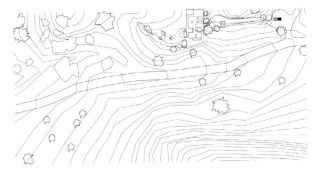

Site plan / Plan de situation

3-D rendering / Représentation en 3D

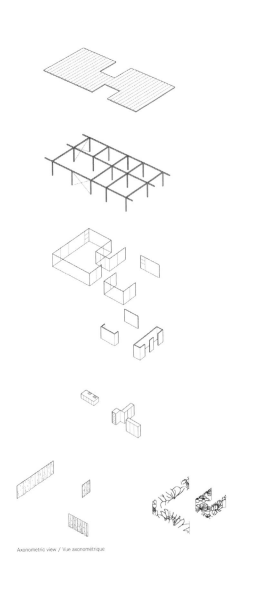

Axonometric view / Vue axonométrique

BRIDGE HOUSE

Max Pritchard Architect
Ashbourne, SA, Australia
© Sam Noonan

The construction system, a concrete slab on a steel structure that crosses over the uneven ground of the land, minimizes the impact on the natural environment. The other measures are thermal and photovoltaic solar panels, a rainwater collection tank and an orientation that favors ventilation and the use of sunlight.

Die Bauweise mit einer Betonplatte auf einer Stahlstruktur, die den Höhenunterschied des Geländes ausgleicht, reduziert die Belastung der natürlichen Umgebung. Wärmekollektoren und Photovoltaikpaneele sowie ein Regenwassertank wurden installiert, und die durchdachte Ausrichtung begünstigt die Belüftung und die Ausnutzung des Tageslichts.

L'originalité de cette maison-pont, qui repose sur une dalle de béton posée sur une structure d'acier, réduit son impact sur l'environnement en préservant le dénivelé du terrain. D'autres mesures ont été adoptées telles l'utilisation de panneaux solaires thermiques et photovoltaïques, un réservoir de collecte des eaux pluviales et l'orientation qui facilite la ventilation et l'exploitation de la lumière solaire.

Het bouwsysteem, een betonnen plaat op een ijzeren structuur waarmee het hoogteverschil van het terrein wordt overwonnen, vermindert de impact op de natuurlijke omgeving. De overige maatregelen zijn thermische en fotovoltaïsche zonnepanelen, een regenopvangtank en een oriëntatie die de ventilatie bevordert en waardoor zonlicht kan worden benut.

El sistema de construcción, una losa de hormigón sobre una estructura de acero que salva el desnivel del terreno, reduce el impacto sobre el entorno natural. Las demás medidas son placas solares térmicas y fotovoltaicas, un tanque de recolección de aguas pluviales y una orientación que favorece la ventilación y el aprovechamiento de la luz solar.

L'idea costruttiva, una lastra in cemento sistemata sopra una struttura in acciaio che preserva il dislivello del terreno, riduce l'impatto sull'ambiente naturale. Le altre scelte riguardano l'uso di pannelli solari termici e fotovoltaici, l'installazione di un serbatoio per la raccolta dell'acqua piovana e un orientamento volto a favorire la ventilazione e lo sfruttamento della luce solare.

O sistema de construção, uma laje de betão sobre uma estrutura de aço que atravessa o desnível do terreno, reduz o impacto sobre o meio natural. As restantes medidas são painéis solares térmicos e fotovoltaicos, um tanque de recolha de águas pluviais e uma orientação que favorece a ventilação e o aproveitamento da luz solar.

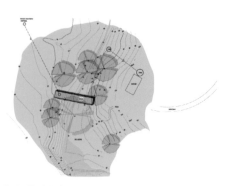

Site plan / Plan de situation

Axonometric of the structure / Axonométrie de la structure

Plan

1. Entrance / Entrée
2. Study – Guestroom / Bureau – Chambre d'amis
3. Laundry / Buanderie
4. Kitchen / Cuisine
5. Living – Dining room / Salon – Salle à manger
6. Bathroom / Salle de bains
7. Bedroom / Chambre

ANNIE RESIDENCE

Bercy Chen Studio
Austin, TX, USA
© Mike Osborne, Joseph Pettyjohn

Out of the all sustainable elements of this home including solar panels and rainwater collection, the insulation and air-conditioning stand out. The latter is achieved through cross ventilation, which creates the windows and movable panels, the vegetation in the central courtyard and the pond, which cools down the atmosphere.

Unter den nachhaltigen Elementen dieses Hauses, das unter anderem mit Sonnenkollektoren und Regenwassertanks ausgestattet ist, sind insbesondere die Isolierung und die Kühlung hervorzuheben. Letztere wird dank Kreuzlüftung über Fenster und bewegliche Paneele, dank der Bepflanzung des Innenhofes und dank des die Luft erfrischenden Teichs erzielt.

Parmi les différentes composantes de développement durable utilisées pour la construction de cette maison, dont les panneaux solaires et la collecte des eaux pluviales, il faut signaler l'isolation et le refroidissement. La climatisation est le résultat de la ventilation croisée obtenue par l'action conjuguée des fenêtres et des panneaux mobiles, de la végétation du patio central et du bassin, qui rafraîchit l'air.

Onder de duurzame elementen die in dit huis aanwezig zijn, zoals de zonnepanelen en de opvang van regenwater, vallen de isolatie en de koeling op. Dit laatste wordt behaald dankzij de kruisventilatie die gecreëerd wordt door de ramen en de mobiele panelen, de vegetatie van de binnenplaats en de vijver die de lucht koelt.

De los elementos sostenibles que incorpora esta casa, entre los que se encuentran los paneles solares y la recogida de aguas pluviales, destacan el aislamiento y la refrigeración. Esta última se consigue gracias a la ventilación cruzada que crean las ventanas y los paneles móviles, a la vegetación del patio central y al estanque, que refresca el aire.

Tra gli elementi sostenibili di cui è dotata questa casa, tra cui i pannelli solari e la raccolta dell'acqua piovana, degni di nota sono l'isolamento e il condizionamento. Quest'ultimo è ottenuto grazie alla ventilazione incrociata prodotta da finestre e pannelli mobili, alla vegetazione del cortile centrale e allo stagno che rinfresca l'aria.

De entre os elementos sustentáveis incorporados nesta casa, nos quais se incluem os painéis solares e o sistema de recolha de águas pluviais, têm especial destaque o isolamento e o arrefecimento. Este último elemento é conseguido graças à ventilação cruzada criada pelas janelas e pelos painéis móveis, à vegetação do pátio central e ao lago, que refresca o ar.

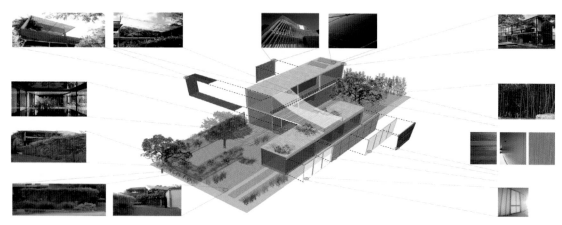

Green features diagram / Croquis des installations écologiques

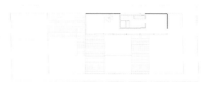

Ground floor / Rez-de-chaussée

Roof plan / Terrasse couverte

FLORIDA BEACH HOUSE

Iredale Pedersen Hook Architects
Florida Beach, WA, Australia
© Iredale Pedersen Hook Architects

This beach house has several passive strategies for saving energy. The glass expanses on the façades are high efficiency and the amount of steel used in the structure has been reduced. The wood used in the interior is recycled for the ceiling or brought in the form of prefabricated panels. The original roof protects from direct sunlight in summer and allows heat through in winter.

Bei diesem Sommerhaus wurden diverse passive Strategien für mehr Energieersparnis eingesetzt. Die Fassadenverglasung ist höchst energieeffizient und der Anteil an verbautem Stahl in der Gebäudestruktur wurde reduziert. Für den Innenraum wurden Recyclingholz und vorgefertigte Paneele eingesetzt. Das originelle Dach schützt im Sommer vor der Sonne und lässt im Winter die Wärme ins Haus.

Cette maison d'été dispose de plusieurs systèmes passifs favorisant les économies d'énergie. Les vitrages des façades sont ultra-performants. L'ossature en acier est des plus économes en matière première. Le bois employé à l'intérieur est recyclé ou a été acheminé sous forme de panneaux préfabriqués. Originale, la toiture protège du soleil en été et laisse la chaleur pénétrer en hiver.

Dit zomerhuis heeft verschillende passieve strategieën om energie te besparen. De glazen van de gevel zijn hoog efficiënt en het gebruik van staal in de structuur is gereduceerd. Het hout in het interieur is gerecycled voor het dak of is in de vorm van geprefabriceerde panelen geleverd. Het originele dak beschermt tegen de zon in de zomer en laat in de winter warmte door.

Esta casa de verano posee varias estrategias pasivas para el ahorro energético. Los cristales de las fachadas son de alta eficiencia y se ha reducido el acero en la estructura. La madera interior es reciclada para la cubierta o traída en forma de paneles prefabricados. El original tejado protege del sol en verano y deja pasar el calor en invierno.

Questa casa estiva adotta varie strategie passive per il risparmio energetico. I vetri delle facciate sono ad alta efficienza energetica ed è stato ridotto l'impiego di acciaio come componente strutturale. Il legno interno per il tetto è riciclato o realizzato sotto forma di pannelli prefabbricati. L'originale copertura protegge dal sole in estate e lascia passare il calore in inverno.

Esta casa de verão possui várias estratégias passivas para a poupança energética. Os vidros das fachadas são de alta eficiência e o uso aço na estrutura foi reduzido. A madeira interior utilizada no tecto é reciclada ou recebida na forma de painéis pré-fabricados. O telhado original protege do sol no Verão e deixa passar o calor no Inverno.

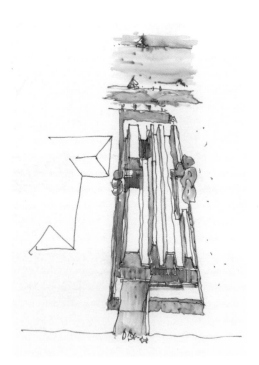

Sketch / Croquis

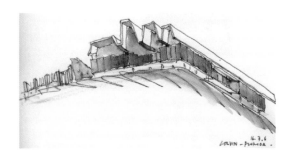

Sketches / Croquis

Elevations / Élévations

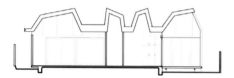

Section / Vue en coupe

Floor plan / Étage

1. Entrance / Entrée
2. Bathroom / Salle de bains
3. Powder / Sanitaires
4. Laundry / Buanderie
5. Playroom / Salle de jeux
6. Garage / Garage
7. Patio / Patio
8. Kitchen / Cuisine
9. Bedroom / Chambre
10. Living room / Salon
11. Dining room / Salle à manger
12. Study / Bureau
13. Dressing room / Dressing

MARTIN LANCASTER

MacKay-Lyons Sweetapple Architects
Prospect, NS, Canada
© Greg Richardson

Awareness of the ecological footprint is the basis of sustainable architecture. If you use the sun for thermal mass and air currents for cross-ventilation, you achieve a better quality of life. ¡In addition, here heat recovery units and flow limiters have been installed, and local vegetation has been planted.

Das Wissen um den ökologischen Fußabdruck bildet die Grundlage des nachhaltigen Bauens. Durch Nutzung der Sonnenenergie zur Wärmespeicherung und der Luftströme für die Kreuzlüftung wird eine Steigerung der Lebensqualität erreicht. In diesem Beispiel wurden außerdem Abwärmeverwerter und Durchflussbegrenzer installiert und es wurde heimische Vegetation angepflanzt.

La prise de conscience de l'empreinte écologique est la base de l'architecture durable. En profitant de la chaleur du soleil pour la masse thermique et de la circulation naturelle de l'air pour la ventilation croisée, on obtient une meilleure qualité de vie. L'installation de récupérateurs de chaleur et de réducteurs de pression complètent ces mesures passives. La végétation plantée est endémique, comme il se doit.

De bewustwording van de ecologische voetafdruk is de grondslag van de duurzame architectuur. Door gebruik te maken van zonlicht voor thermische massa en de luchtstromen te gebruiken voor kruisventilatie, wordt een betere levenskwaliteit mogelijk. Bovendien zijn er warmte-terugwinsystemen en debietregelaars ingebouwd en is de beplanting van plaatselijke oorsprong.

La conciencia de la huella ecológica es la base de la arquitectura sostenible. Si se aprovecha el sol para la masa térmica y las corrientes de aire para la ventilación cruzada, se consigue una mejor calidad de vida. Además, aquí se han instalado recuperadores de calor y limitadores de caudal y se ha plantado vegetación de origen local.

La consapevolezza dell'impronta ecologica è la base dell'architettura sostenibile. Sfruttando il sole per la massa termica e le correnti d'aria per la ventilazione incrociata, si ottiene una migliore qualità della vita. Inoltre qui sono stati installati dei dispositivi per il recupero del calore e dei limitatori di flusso ed è stata piantata della vegetazione di origine locale.

A consciência da pegada ecológica é a base da arquitectura sustentável. Ao aproveitar o sol para massa térmica e as correntes de ar para a ventilação cruzada, é conseguida uma melhor qualidade de vida. Adicionalmente, aqui foram instalados recuperadores de calor e limitadores de caudal e foi plantada vegetação de origem local.

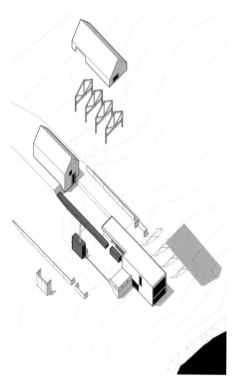

Axonometric view / Vue axonométrique

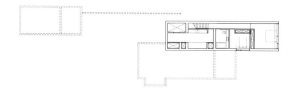

Basement floor / Sous-sol

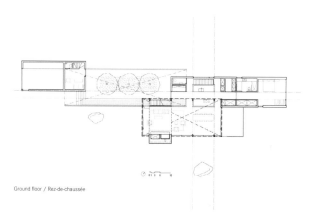

Ground floor / Rez-de-chaussée

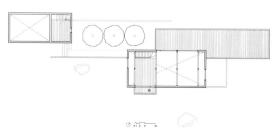

Second floor / Premier étage

CASA TUNQUEN

Riesco + Rivera Arquitectos Asociados
Tunquen, Casablanca, Chile
© Sebastián Melo and Carlos Eguiguren

The choice of the materials that are used in the construction of a house can represent a major reduction in CO_2 emissions. Local materials require less transport, and natural or recycled materials less CO_2 manufacturing processes. In this home, practically all the wooden panels from the siding are reused.

Durch eine wohlüberlegte Auswahl der Baumaterialien kann der CO_2-Ausstoß beachtlich gesenkt werden. Lokale Baustoffe erfordern weniger Transport, natürliche und recycelte Materialien verursachen weniger CO_2-Emissionen bei der Produktion. Nahezu alle für die Verkleidung dieses Wohnhauses verwendeten Holzleisten wurden wiederverwertet.

Le choix des matériaux employés dans la construction d'une maison peut se traduire par une importante baisse des émissions de CO_2. L'origine locale des matériaux réduit les coûts liés au transport, et les processus de transformation des matériaux naturels ou recyclés génèrent moins de CO_2. Presque tout le bois utilisé pour les revêtements de cette demeure connaît une seconde vie.

De juiste materiaalkeuze bij de bouw van een huis kan de CO_2-uitstoot aanzienlijk verlagen. Het gebruik van plaatselijke materialen betekent minder vervoer en door natuurlijke of gerecyclede materialen ontstaat er minder CO_2 tijdens het fabricageproces. In deze woning zijn praktisch alle houten panelen voor de bekleding gerecycled.

La elección de los materiales que se usan en la construcción de una casa puede representar una importante reducción de emisiones de CO_2. Los materiales locales implican menor transporte, y los naturales o reciclados, menos CO_2 derivado de los procesos de fabricación. En esta residencia, prácticamente todos los paneles de madera del revestimiento son reutilizados.

La scelta dei materiali usati nella costruzione di una casa può incidere in modo significativo nella riduzione delle emissioni di CO_2. L'uso di materiali locali implica meno trasporti mentre la scelta di materiali naturali o riciclati si traduce nella riduzione delle emissioni di CO_2 collegate ai processi produttivi. In questa casa praticamente tutti i pannelli di legno del rivestimento sono riciclati.

A escolha dos materiais que se usam na construção de uma casa pode representar uma importante redução de emissões de CO_2. Os materiais locais implicam menos transporte, e os naturais ou reciclados, menos CO_2 de processos de fabrico. Nesta residência, praticamente todos os painéis de madeira do revestimento provêm de reutilização.

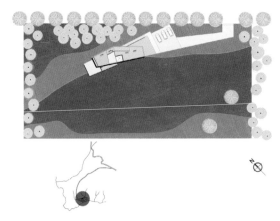

Location plan / Plan de situation

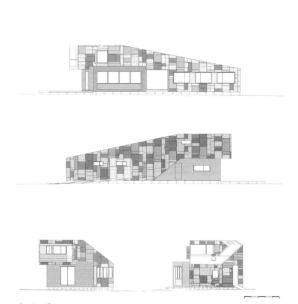

Elevations / Élévations

Ground floor / Rez-de-chaussée

Roof plan / Toiture en terrasse couverte

Second floor / Premier étage

1. Entrance / Entrée
2. Laundry room / Buanderie
3. Kitchen / Cuisine
4. Dining room / Salle à manger
5. Living room / Salon
6. Green patio / Patio vert
7. Bedroom / Chambre

8. Bathroom / Salle de bains
9. Terrace / Terrasse
10. Main bedroom / Chambre principale
11. Dressing room / Dressing
12. Main bathroom / Salle de bains principale
13. Terrace / Terrasse

a-a

b-b

c-c

d-d

f-f

e-e

Sections / Vues en coupe

AIR HOUSE

Francois Perrin
Brentwood, CA, USA
© Michaels Wells, Joshua White

The second polycarbonate skin that covers the wooden façade of this extension fulfils an insulating function, as it acts as an air chamber that creates a greenhouse effect. The orientation of the house promotes ventilation and solar panels on the roof and mini wind turbines provide the required electric energy.

Die zweite Haut aus Polycarbonat, die die hölzerne Fassade dieses Ausbaus verkleidet, dient – da sie eine Luftkammer mit Wintergarteneffekt erzeugt – als Wärmedämmung. Die Ausrichtung des Hauses sorgt für eine gute Belüftung, während auf dem Dach installierte Sonnenkollektoren und einige Mikro-Windkraftanlagen die erforderliche elektrische Energie erzeugen.

La deuxième peau de polycarbonate qui double la façade en bois de cet agrandissement joue un rôle d'isolant, en fonctionnant comme un vide d'air qui génère un effet de serre. L'orientation de la maison favorise la ventilation. Les panneaux solaires de la toiture et les mini-éoliennes fournissent toute l'électricité nécessaire aux habitants.

De tweede huid van policarbonaat waarmee de houten gevel van deze uitbouw bekleed is, heeft een isolerende functie, aangezien hij dienst doet als een luchtkamer waarmee een broeikaseffect teweeg wordt gebracht. De oriëntatie van het huis bevordert de ventilatie en enkele zonnepanelen op het dak en micro-windgeneratoren leveren de nodige energie.

La segunda piel de policarbonato que reviste la fachada de madera de esta ampliación cumple con una función aislante, al actuar como una cámara de aire que genera un efecto invernadero. La orientación de la casa favorece la ventilación y unos paneles solares en la cubierta y unos microgeneradores eólicos proporcionan la energía eléctrica necesaria.

La seconda pelle in policarbonato che riveste la facciata in legno di questo ampliamento svolge una funzione isolante agendo come una camera d'aria che genera un effetto serra. L'orientamento della casa favorisce la ventilazione; alcuni pannelli solari sul tetto e dei microgeneratori eolici forniscono l'energia elettrica necessaria.

A segunda pele de policarbonato que reveste a fachada de madeira desta ampliação desempenha uma função isolante uma vez que funciona como uma câmara de ar que gera um efeito de estufa. A orientação da casa favorece a ventilação e os painéis solares e os microgeradores eólicos no telhado proporcionam a energia eléctrica necessária.

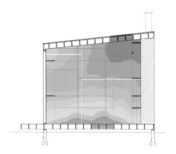
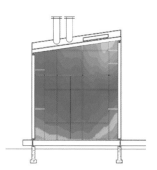
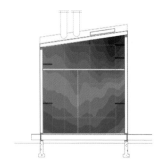
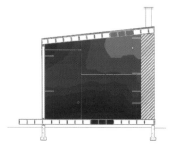

Diagrams showing energy peaks during the seasonal cycle / Diagrammes montrant les fluctuations saisonnières de la température

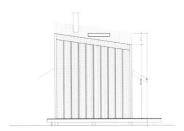

North elevation / Élévation nord

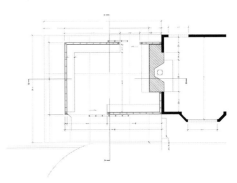

Floor plan / Étage

LEICESTER HOUSE

SPG Architects
Leicester, NC, USA
© Charles Lindsay

Combining aesthetics, functionality and energy efficiency is the objective of this home. A geothermal climate system control energy consumption and collects 80% of rainwater for lavatories and gardens reduce water consumption. The green roof in one part of the house contributes to the thermal insulation of the interior.

Bei diesem Haus sollten Ästhetik, Funktionalität und Energieeffizienz vereint werden. Ein Erdwärme-Klimasystem senkt den Energieverbrauch, und durch das Auffangen von 80 % des Regenwassers für Toilettenspülung und Gartenbewässerung wird auch der Wasserverbrauch reduziert. Das bepflanzte Dach über einem Teil des Hauses trägt zu einer besseren Wärmedämmung bei.

Les concepteurs de ce logement souhaitaient fusionner esthétique, fonctionnalité et efficacité énergétique. La climatisation géothermique permet la maîtrise de la dépense en énergie tandis que la collecte de 80 % des eaux pluviales pour l'usage sanitaire et les jardins réduit la consommation d'eau. La toiture végétale d'une partie de la maison contribue à l'isolation thermique de l'intérieur.

Het combineren van esthetiek, functionaliteit en energetische efficiëntie is de doelstelling van deze woning. Een geothermisch luchtbehandelingssysteem houdt de energiekosten laag en 80% van het regenwater wordt opgevangen en gebruikt voor de wc en de tuinen, waardoor het waterverbruik minder is. Het met planten begroeide dak op een deel van het huis draagt bij aan warmte-isolatie binnen.

Unir estética, funcionalidad y eficiencia energética es el objetivo de esta vivienda. Un sistema de climatización geotérmica controla el gasto energético y la recolección del 80% del agua de lluvia para inodoros y jardines reduce el consumo de agua. La cubierta vegetal en una parte de la casa contribuye al aislamiento térmico del interior.

Unire estetica, funzionalità ed efficienza energetica è l'obiettivo di questa abitazione. Un sistema di climatizzazione geotermica consente di contenere le spese energetiche mentre il recupero dell'80% dell'acqua piovana per lo scarico del water e l'irrigazione del giardino riduce il consumo di acqua. L'uso di un rivestimento vegetale in una parte della casa contribuisce all'isolamento termico interno.

Unir estética, funcionalidade e eficiência energética é o objectivo desta habitação. Um sistema de climatização geotérmica controla o consumo energético e a recolha de 80% da água da chuva para uso nas casas de banho e nos jardins reduz o consumo de água. A cobertura vegetal numa parte da casa contribui para o isolamento térmico do interior.

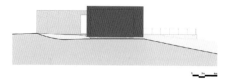

North elevation / Élévation nord

South elevation / Élévation sud

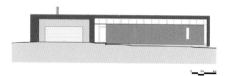

East elevation / Élévation est

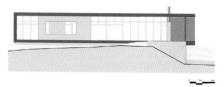

West elevation / Élévation ouest

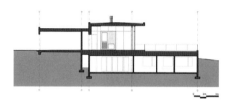

South section / Vue en coupe sud

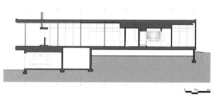

West section / Vue en coupe ouest

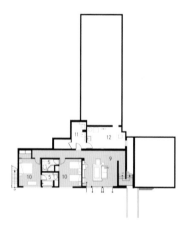

Ground floor / Rez-de-chaussée

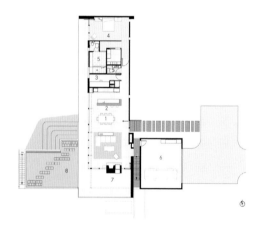

Second floor / Premier étage

1. Dining-living room / Salon - salle à manger
2. Kitchen / Cuisine
3. Study / Bureau
4. Master bedroom / Chambre principale
5. Bathroom / Salle de bains
6. Garage / Garage
7. Outdoor dining / Salon extérieur
8. Green roof / Couverture végétale
9. Living room / Salle de séjour
10. Bedroom / Chambre
11. Laundry / Buanderie
12. Mechanical room / Pièce technique

MOSMAN HOUSE

Popov Bass Architects
Mosman, NSW, Australia
© Alex Popov, Kurt Arnold, Kraig Carlstrom

In a large house, the consumption of natural resources should be controlled. Therefore, in this home materials that required zero maintenance were used, as were LED lights and flow regulator faucets. Rainwater is collected for irrigation, the washing machine, the bathrooms and the pool, which is heated with solar energy. Photovoltaic panels supply electricity.

In einem großen Haus muss der Verbrauch natürlicher Ressourcen minimiert werden. Daher kamen hier wartungsfreie Materialien, LEDs und Durchflussbegrenzer zum Einsatz. Regenwasser wird aufgefangen und für Bewässerung, Waschmaschine, Bäder und den mit Solarenergie beheizten Swimmingpool verwendet. Photovoltaikpaneele erzeugen elektrische Energie.

Dans une grande maison, il faut maîtriser la consommation de ressources naturelles, d'où une prédilection certaine pour des matériaux qui ne demandent pas d'entretien, comme ceux choisis ici. Les éclairages à leds et les robinets munis de réducteur de débit contribuent à cet effort. Les eaux de pluie collectées sont utilisées pour l'arrosage, la machine à laver, les sanitaires et la piscine, chauffée par l'énergie solaire. Les panneaux photovoltaïques produisent l'électricité.

In een groot huis moet het verbruik van natuurlijke hulpbronnen in de gaten worden gehouden. Zo zijn er in deze woning onderhoudsvrije materialen gebruikt en zijn er led-lampen en kranen met debietregelaars geïnstalleerd. Regenwater wordt opgevangen en gebruikt voor besproeiing, de wasmachine, badkamers en het zwembad, dat verwarmd wordt met zonne-energie. De fotovoltaïsche panelen leveren de elektriciteit.

En una casa grande debe controlarse el consumo de recursos naturales. Así, en esta vivienda se usaron materiales que no requerían mantenimiento, luces led y grifos reguladores de caudal. Se recupera el agua de lluvia para el riego, la lavadora, los baños y la piscina, donde se calienta con energía solar. Los paneles fotovoltaicos proporcionan la electricidad.

In una casa di grandi dimensioni è necessario tenere sotto controllo il consumo di risorse naturali. In questa abitazione sono stati impiegati materiali che non richiedono manutenzione, luci a led e rubinetti con riduttori di flusso. Viene recuperata l'acqua piovana per l'irrigazione, la lavatrice, i bagni e la piscina, dove viene riscaldata con l'energia solare. I pannelli fotovoltaici forniscono l'elettricità.

Numa casa grande deve controlar-se o consumo de recursos naturais. Assim, nesta habitação foram usados materiais que não requerem manutenção, luzes led e torneiras com regulador de caudal. A água da chuva é recuperada para a rega, máquina de lavar roupa, casas de banho e piscina, sendo esta aquecida com energia solar. Os painéis fotovoltaicos proporcionam a electricidade.

Location plan / Plan de situation

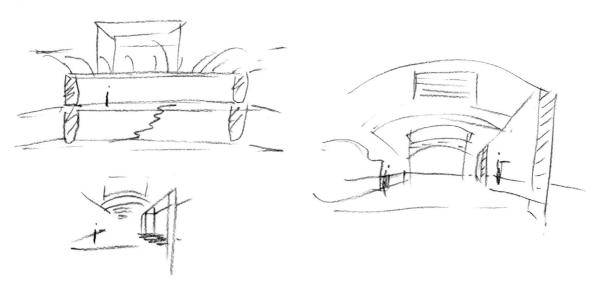

Sketches / Croquis

Lower level / Niveau inférieur

Main level / Niveau principal

Upper level / Niveau supérieur

1. Entrance / Entrée
2. Living room / Salon
3. Family room / Séjour
4. Dining room / Salle à manger
5. Kitchen / Cuisine
6. Master bedroom / Chambre principale
7. Dressing room / Dressing
8. Main bathroom / Salle de bains principale
9. Porch / Porche
10. Terrace / Terrasse
11. Bedroom / Chambre
12. Bathroom / Salle de bains
13. Storage / Rangements
14. Garage / Garage
15. Study / Bureau
16. Pool / Piscine
17. Playroom / Salle de jeux

HOUSE IN OREGON COAST

Obie G. Bowman
Gold Beach, OR, USA
© Obie Bowman

This small cabin was designed to resist strong winds and the harsh climatic conditions in the area. Self-sufficiency was another objective. Resistant materials such as local wood were used and photovoltaic panels were installed. A tank is used to collect rainwater, which supplements the water obtained from a well.

Beim Entwurf dieser kleinen Hütte wurde darauf geachtet, dass sie den starken Winden und widrigen Klimabedingungen der Gegend standhält. Ein weiteres Ziel bestand darin, einen energieautarken Bau zu kreieren. Es wurden widerstandsfähige Materialien wie lokale Hölzer verbaut und Photovoltaikpaneele installiert. Ein Regenwassertank ergänzt die aus einem Brunnen gewonnene Wassermenge.

Cette petite cabane est conçue pour résister aux vents violents et aux conditions climatiques rigoureuses sur cette côte. Il fallait également qu'elle soit autonome. On a utilisé des matériaux résistants, comme le bois local, et installé des panneaux photovoltaïques. Un réservoir collecte les eaux pluviales venant compléter le puits pour l'approvisionnement en eau.

Deze kleine hut is zo ontworpen dat het bestand is tegen de harde wind en de zware weersomstandigheden van het gebied. De zelfvoorziening voor wat betreft natuurlijke hulpbronnen is een andere doelstelling. Er zijn resistente materialen gebruikt zoals uit de omgeving afkomstig hout en er zijn fotovoltaïsche panelen geïnstalleerd. Het water wordt verkregen door een regenopvangtank en uit een put.

Esta pequeña cabaña se diseñó para resistir los fuertes vientos y las duras condiciones climáticas de la zona. La autosuficiencia de recursos era otro objetivo. Se utilizaron materiales resistentes como la madera local y se instalaron paneles fotovoltaicos. Un tanque de recogida de agua pluvial, junto a un pozo, abastecen de agua.

Questa piccola capanna è stata progettata per resistere ai forti venti e alle rigide condizioni climatiche della zona. L'autosufficienza in termini di risorse era un altro obiettivo. Sono stati utilizzati materiali resistenti come il legno locale e sono stati installati alcuni pannelli fotovoltaici. L'acqua piovana, raccolta in un apposito serbatoio, va ad aggiungersi a quella estratta da un pozzo.

Esta pequena cabana foi concebida para resistir aos fortes ventos e às duras condições climatéricas da zona. A auto-suficiência de recursos era outro objectivo pretendido. Foram utilizados materiais resistentes como a madeira local e foram instalados painéis fotovoltaicos. Um tanque de recolha de água pluvial complementa a oferta de água proporcionada por um poço.

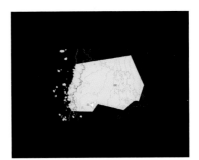

Site plan / Plan de situation

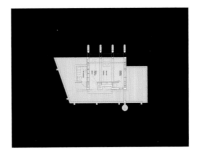

Plan / Étage

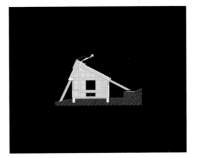

Cross section / Coupe transversale

ADDITION TO MARTIN RESIDENCE

Jason Langkammerer, John Barone/@6 Architecture
Berkeley, CA, USA
© Adrian Gregorutti

This extension that adds a bedroom and a living room to the original house has been clad in fiber-cement siding. The design of this siding has several advantages: the use of less material, ventilated façade to prevent fungus and plagues and low-maintenance. The orientation and a thermal chimney help the air-conditioning of the interior.

Dieser Anbau, der dem ursprünglichen Haus ein weiteres Schlafzimmer und einen Salon schenkte, wurde mit Faserzementplatten verkleidet. Dieses Design hat folgende Vorteile: Es wird weniger Baumaterial verbraucht, die Fassade ist zum Schutz vor Schimmel und Insekten ausreichend belüftet und sie erfordert nur eine sehr geringe Wartung. Die Ausrichtung und der durchdachte Kamineffekt tragen zur Klimatisierung des Inneren des Hauses bei.

L'ensemble, composé d'une chambre et d'un salon, construit pour agrandir la maison initiale, a été recouvert de panneaux en fibrociment. Cet habillage présente plusieurs avantages : économie du matériaux utilisé, ventilation de la façade évitant la formation de moisissures et de mousses. Il demande donc peu d'entretien. L'orientation et une cheminée thermique contribuent à la climatisation.

Deze woning, waarbij een extra slaapkamer en een salon aan het bestaande huis zijn aangebouwd, is omhuld met vezelcementen panelen. Het ontwerp van deze bekleding omvat verschillende voordelen: er hoeft minder materiaal te worden gebruik; ventilatie van de gevel, zodat schimmel en ongedierte worden voorkomen en weinig onderhoud. De oriëntatie en een thermische schoorsteen helpen bij de luchtbehandeling van het interieur.

Esta ampliación, que suma un dormitorio y un salón a la casa original, se ha cubierto de paneles de fibrocemento. El diseño del revestimiento supone varias ventajas: uso de una menor cantidad de material, fachada ventilada para evitar hongos y plagas, y escaso mantenimiento. La orientación y una chimenea térmica ayudan a la climatización del interior.

Questo ampliamento, che aggiunge una camera e una sala alla struttura originaria, è avvolto da pannelli in fibrocemento. Questo tipo di rivestimento offre molteplici vantaggi: uso di una minore quantità di materiale, facciata ventilata per evitare funghi e parassiti riducendo gli interventi di manutenzione. L'orientamento e un camino termico contribuiscono alla climatizzazione degli ambienti interni.

Esta ampliação, que adiciona um quarto e uma sala à casa original, foi envolvida em painéis de fibrocimento. O design do revestimento implica várias vantagens: uso de uma menor quantidade de material, fachada ventilada para evitar fungos e pragas e manutenção mínima. A orientação e a chaminé térmica contribuem para a climatização do interior.

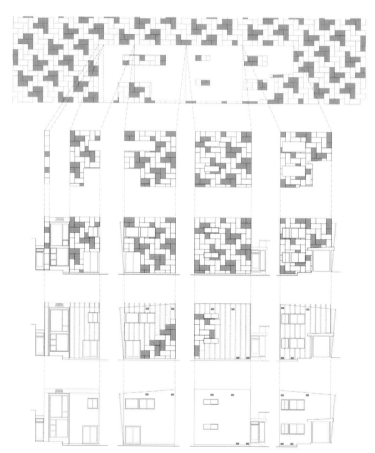

Diagram of fiber-cement cladding / Croquis du revêtement en plaque de fibrociment

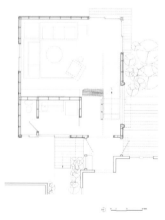

Ground floor / Rez-de-chaussée

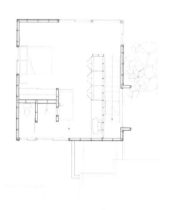

Second floor / Premier étage

SUSTAINABLE RESIDENCE

Dan Rockhill/Studio 804
Kansas City, KS, USA
© Courtesy of Studio 804

Studio 804 is a training program from the Kansas State University of Architecture and Planning in which the students carry out a sustainable project that meets the requirements to obtain the prestigious LEED home certification. This project shows the active and passive strategies, controlled materials and the most common water reuse systems.

Studio 804 ist ein Ausbildungsprogramm des Fachbereichs Architektur und Stadtplanung an der Universität Kansas, in dessen Rahmen die Studenten ein nachhaltiges Projekt entwerfen, das sämtliche Kriterien erfüllen muss, um die renommierte LEED-Zertifizierung für Wohngebäude zu erhalten. Bei diesem Projekt kamen aktive und passive Nachhaltigkeitsstrategien, Materialien mit kontrollierter Herkunft und die üblicherweise verwendeten Wasserwiederverwertungssysteme zum Einsatz.

Studio 804 est un programme de formation de l'Université d'Architecture et de Planification Urbaine du Kansas. Les étudiants doivent réaliser un projet durable répondant au cahier des charges qui permet l'obtention de la prestigieuse certification LEED pour l'architecture résidentielle. Ce projet utilise les stratégies actives et passives, des matériaux contrôlés et les installations habituelles pour la réutilisation de l'eau.

Studio 804 is een onderwijsprogramma van de Universiteit van Bouwkunde en Planologie van Kansas, waar de studenten een duurzaam project uitwerken dat voldoet aan de vereisten om de prestigieuze LEED-kwalificatie van woonarchitectuur te behalen. Dit project omvat de meest voorkomende actieve en passieve strategieën, gecontroleerde materialen en systemen voor het hergebruik van water.

Studio 804 es un programa formativo de la Universidad de Arquitectura y Planificación Urbanística de Kansas en el que los estudiantes realizan un proyecto sostenible que cumpla los requisitos para obtener la prestigiosa calificación LEED de arquitectura residencial. Este proyecto utiliza las estrategias activas y pasivas, los materiales controlados y los sistemas de reutilización de agua más habituales.

Studio 804 è un programma formativo dell'Università di architettura e pianificazione urbanistica del Kansas in cui gli studenti realizzano un progetto sostenibile che soddisfi i requisiti necessari a ottenere la prestigiosa certificazione LEED per l'architettura residenziale. Questo progetto illustra le strategie attive e passive, i controlli sui materiali e i sistemi più comuni di riutilizzo dell'acqua.

Studio 804 é um programa de formação da Universidade de Arquitectura e Planificação Urbanística do Kansas no qual os estudantes realizam um projecto sustentável que cumpra os requisitos necessários para obter a prestigiosa classificação LEED de arquitectura residencial. Este projecto apresenta as estratégias activas e passivas, os materiais controlados e os sistemas de reutilização de água mais habituais.

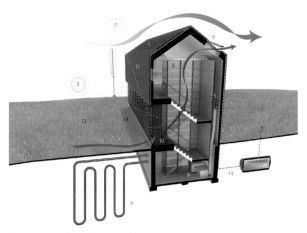

Diagram of environmental features / Croquis des installations écologiques

1. Photovoltaic solar panels / Panneaux solaires photovoltaïques
2. Hydronic radiant floor / Sol radiant hydronique
3. Residential wind turbine / Éolienne
4. Geothermal heat pump / Pompe à chaleur géothermique
5. High efficiency HVAC / Climatisation efficace
6. Energy recovery ventilator / Échangeur de chaleur
7. Passive solar design / Orientation solaire passive

8. Steel and glass stair core / Escalier en acier et verre
9. Cross ventilation / Ventilation croisée
10. Concrete thermal massing / Masse thermique de béton
11. FSC Certified Tropical wood rainscreen (FSC) / Bois tropical certifié (FSC)
12. High performance glazing system / Verre à haut rendement
13. Draught tolerant landscaping / Végétation résistante à la sécheresse
14. Rainwater harvesting systems / Système de captation des eaux pluviales

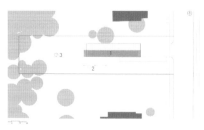

Site plan / Plan de situation

1. Rooftop solar panels / Panneaux solaires sur la toiture
2. Geothermal heat wells / Puits d'énergie géothermique
3. Wind turbine / Éolienne

Plans / Étages

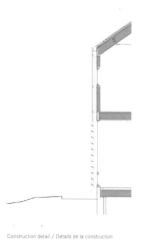

Construction detail / Détails de la construction

CABIN ON FLATHEAD LAKE

Andersson Wise Architects
Polson, MT, USA
© Art M. Gray

Erecting the cabin on six pillars anchored to concrete foundations has meant that the natural environment of these important forests in Montana have been respected, as they are the natural habitat of Ospreys. In addition, many of the elements were assembled far from the house, thereby reducing the alteration of the land.

Dank der Tatsache, dass diese Hütte auf sechs in Betonfundamente eingelassenen Pfeilern errichtet wurde, konnten die umgebenden Wälder des US-Bundesstaats Montana, die einen wichtigen Lebensraum für den Fischadler darstellen, so weit wie möglich geschont werden. Ferner wurden zahlreiche Elemente in gewisser Entfernung vom Haus platziert, wodurch das Gelände noch weniger beeinträchtigt wurde.

La solution consistant à construire cette cabane sur six piliers ancrés dans un socle en ciment de béton garantissait le respect de l'environnement naturel des forêts du Montana, où nichent des balbuzards pêcheurs. L'enjeu était donc essentiel. Par ailleurs, de nombreux éléments ont été assemblés loin du site pour limiter au maximum les effets de la construction sur le terrain.

Met de oplossing voor de bouw van deze hut, die rust op een fundering van zes in beton verankerde pilaren, is de natuurlijke omgeving van de bossen van Montana zo veel mogelijk intact gehouden. Deze omgeving heeft een grote waarde doordat het het leefgebied is van visarenden. Bovendien zijn de elementen ver van het huis gemonteerd, waardoor het terrein nog minder hoeft te worden gewijzigd.

La solución de construir la cabaña sobre seis pilares anclados en cimientos de hormigón ha permitido respetar al máximo el entorno natural de estos bosques de Montana, de gran importancia por ser el hábitat de águilas pescadoras. Además, muchos de los elementos se montaron lejos de la casa, por lo que la alteración del terreno se redujo aún más.

La soluzione di costruire la capanna su sei pilastri ancorati a basi in cemento armato ha consentito di rispettare al massimo l'ambiente naturale di questi boschi del Montana, prezioso rifugio e habitat delle aquile pescatrici. Inoltre, molti elementi sono stati assemblati lontano dalla casa, riducendo ulteriormente l'alterazione del terreno.

A solução encontrada de construir a cabana sobre seis pilares ancorados sobre fundações de betão permitiu respeitar ao máximo o meio natural desta floresta muito importante no Montana uma vez que se trata do habitat de águias-pesqueiras. Adicionalmente, muitos dos elementos foram montados longe da casa, o que permitiu reduzir ainda mais as alterações no terreno.

Location plan / Plan de situation

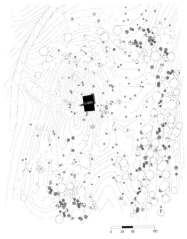

Site plan / Plan de la parcelle

Section / Vue en coupe

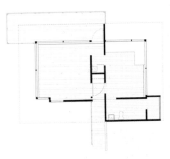

Plan / Étage

HOUSE IN THE SAND

Aires Mateus e Asociados
Comporta, Grândola, Portugal
© Aires Mateus

The recovery of the buildings encourages the re-use of materials, in this case reinforced by the use of natural materials: wood and straw roofs. The traditional architecture adapts to the climate of the area and the location of the rooms in the existing pavilions creates a poetic space with minimal impact on nature.

Der Wiedergewinnung bestehender Gebäude liegt der fest Wille für eine neue Nutzung zugrunde. In diesem Falle ist der Einsatz natürlicher Materialien – Holz und Strohdächer – hervorzuheben. Die auf dem traditionellen Stil basierende Bauweise wurde an das Klima der Region angepasst, und durch die Unterbringung der Zimmer in den bestehenden Pavillons entsteht ein poetischer Raum mit minimaler Umweltbelastung.

La réhabilitation des bâtiments s'accompagne d'une volonté de réutilisation des matériaux, soulignée ici par l'emploi en complément de matériaux naturels : bois et toitures de paille. L'architecture fidèle à la tradition s'est adaptée au climat de la zone, et l'implantation des pièces dans les pavillons pré-existants crée un espace poétique à très faible impact sur la nature.

Uit de herstelwerkzaamheden die aan de gebouwen zijn uitgevoerd, blijkt het voornemen om te recyclen; in dit geval wordt dit bevestigd door het gebruik van natuurlijke materialen: hout en rieten daken. De op traditie gestoelde architectuur past zich aan het klimaat van de regio aan en dankzij de indeling van de vertrekken in de bestaande paviljoens ontstaat een poëtische ruimte met zo weinig mogelijk impact op de natuur.

La recuperación de los edificios implica una voluntad de reaprovechamiento, en este caso reafirmada por el uso de materiales naturales: madera y cubiertas de paja. La arquitectura basada en la tradición se adapta al clima de la zona, y la ubicación de las estancias en los pabellones existentes crea un espacio poético con un impacto mínimo en la naturaleza.

Il recupero degli edifici implica una volontà di rivalorizzazione, in questo caso rafforzata dall'uso di materiali naturali: legno e tetti di paglia. L'architettura basata sulla tradizione si adatta al clima della zona e l'ubicazione degli ambienti nei padiglioni esistenti crea uno spazio poetico con un impatto minimo sul contesto naturale.

A recuperação dos edifícios implica uma vontade de reaproveitar materiais, neste caso reforçada pelo uso de materiais naturais: madeira e telhados de palha. A arquitectura baseada na tradição adapta-se ao clima da zona, e a localização das divisões nos pavilhões existentes cria um espaço poético com um impacto mínimo na natureza.

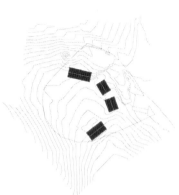

Location plan / Plan de situation

Sections / Vue en coupe

Elevations / Élévations

Construction details / Détails de la construction

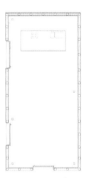

Communal spaces plan / Étage des pièces de vie

Bedrooms plan / Étage des chambres

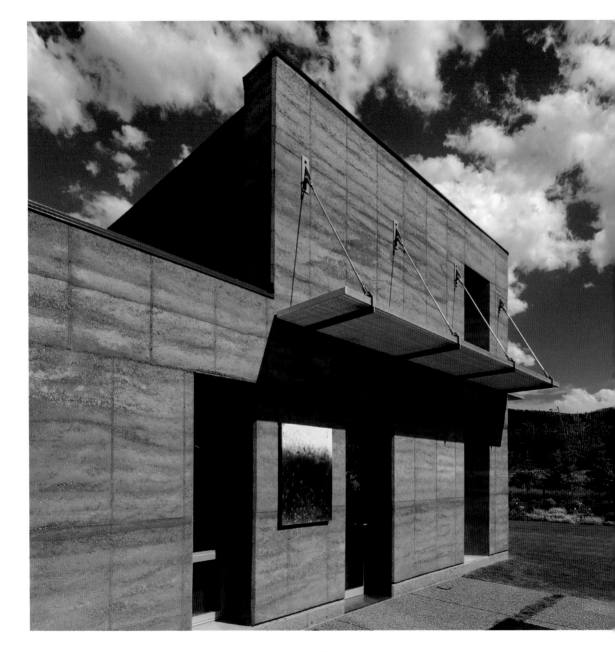

LORD

Studio B Architects
Aspen, CO, USA
© Aspen Architectural Photography, Paul Warchol

This house stands out for its use of compacted soil, which reduces CO_2 emissions as it comes from local land. Other measures adopted to achieve better energy efficiency are the use of flow regulators and low consumption lamps. Also, low-e windows have been installed that limit the heat that enters.

Dieses Haus zeichnet sich durch die Verwendung von verdichtetem Lehm aus lokalen Böden aus, der für eine Verringerung des CO_2-Ausstoßes sorgt. Um eine bessere Energieeffizienz zu erzielen, wurden außerdem Durchflussbegrenzer und Energiesparlampen installiert. Die verbauten Low-E-Fenster begrenzen das Eindringen von Wärme in das Haus.

Cette maison en terre compactée d'origine locale, dont l'usage a permis de réduire les émissions de CO_2 du chantier, est remarquable. Dans le cadre d'une plus grande efficacité énergétique, il faut signaler dans les équipements les robinets à régulateur de pression et les ampoules basse consommation. De plus, les vitrages à basse émissivité réduisent la pénétration de la chaleur.

Dit huis valt op door het gebruik van compacte aarde, waardoor de CO_2-uitstoot vermindert, doordat het afkomstig is uit de plaatselijke bodem. Andere maatregelen die genomen zijn voor een betere energie-efficiënte zijn het gebruik van debietregelaars en van spaarlampen. Bovendien zijn er *low-e*-ramen geïnstalleerd, waardoor minder warmte wordt binnengelaten.

Esta casa destaca por el uso de la tierra compactada, que reduce las emisiones de CO_2 al proceder del suelo local. Otras de las medidas que se han adoptado para lograr una mayor eficiencia energética son el empleo de reguladores de caudal y de lámparas de bajo consumo. Además, se han instalado cristales Low-e, que limitan la entrada de calor en el interior.

Questa casa si impone per l'uso della terra compattata, che riduce le emissioni di CO_2 dato che proviene da terreni circostanti. Altre scelte volte a ottenere una maggiore efficienza energetica sono l'utilizzo di regolatori di flusso e di lampadine a basso consumo. Sono stati inoltre installati vetri *low-e* (a basso emissivo), che limitano l'ingresso del calore all'interno della struttura.

Esta casa destaca-se pelo uso de terra compactada, que reduz as emissões de CO_2 visto proceder do solo local. Outras medidas que foram aplicadas para obter uma maior eficiência energética incluíram a utilização de reguladores de caudal e lâmpadas de baixo consumo. Adicionalmente, foram instalados vidros *low-e*, que limitam a entrada de calor no interior.

Location plan / Plan de situation

Ground floor / Rez-de-chaussée

Second floor / Premier étage

N+C TOWNHOUSE

Studio 101 Architects
Geelong, VIC, Australia
© Trevor Mein/Meinphoto

In the N+C Townhouse traditional materials are combined with other low VOC materials and with recycled wood, especially in the interior cladding. The courtyard facilitates cross ventilation and double-glazed windows with argon gas improve insulation. A few underground tanks collect rainwater and graywater is reused for irrigation.

Beim N+C Townhouse wurden traditionelle Baustoffe mit Recyclingholz (insbesondere bei der Innenverkleidung) und Materialien kombiniert, die einen niedrigen Gehalt an flüchtigen organischen Verbindungen aufweisen. Der Innenhof erleichtert die Kreuzlüftung und die Fenster mit Argon-Doppelverglasung verbessern die Wärmedämmung. Unterirdische Tanks fangen das Regenwasser auf und das Grauwasser wird für die Bewässerung des Gartens verwendet.

La résidence N+C associe matériaux traditionnels et matériaux à faible contenu en composés organiques volatils et en bois recyclé, notamment pour les revêtements intérieurs. Le patio facilite la ventilation croisée et les fenêtres à double vitrage avec lame d'argon améliorent l'isolation. Des réservoirs enterrés recueillent les eaux pluviales tandis que les eaux grises sont recyclées pour l'arrosage.

In het N+C huis worden traditionele materialen gecombineerd met andere materialen met een laag gehalte aan organische vluchtige organische stoffen en gerecycled hout, met name voor de binnenbekleding. De binnenplaats verbetert de kruisventilatie en de ramen met dubbel glas met argongas zorgen voor een betere isolatie. Het regenwater wordt opgevangen in enkele tanks onder de grond. Voor de besproeiing wordt grijs water hergebruikt.

En la residencia N+C se combinan materiales tradicionales con otros con bajo contenido en compuestos orgánicos volátiles y con madera reciclada, sobre todo en el revestimiento interior. El patio facilita la ventilación cruzada y las ventanas de doble vidrio con gas argón mejoran el aislamiento. Unos tanques subterráneos recogen el agua de lluvia y para el riego se reutilizan las aguas grises.

Nella N+C materiali tradizionali si alternano ad altri a basso contenuto di composti organici volatili e a base di legno riciclato, soprattutto nel rivestimento esterno. Il cortile facilita la ventilazione incrociata e le finestre con doppi vetri contenenti argon migliorano l'isolamento. Dei serbatoi sotterranei raccolgono l'acqua piovana e per l'irrigazione vengono riutilizzate le acque grigie.

Na casa N+C são combinados materiais tradicionais com outros de baixo teor em compostos orgânicos voláteis e com madeira reciclada, sobretudo no revestimento interior. O pátio facilita a ventilação cruzada e as janelas de vidro duplo com gás árgon melhoram o isolamento. Tanques subterrâneos recolhem a água da chuva e as águas cinzentas são reutilizadas para rega.

Site plan / Plan de la parcelle

Ground floor / Rez-de-chaussée

Second floor / Premier étage

1. Entrance / Entrée
2. Bedroom / Chambre
3. Bathroom / Salle de bains
4. Laundry / Buanderie
5. Play room / Salle de jeux
6. Patio / Patio

7. Dining room / Salle à manger
8. Living room / Salon
9. Terrace / Terrasse
10. Kitchen / Cuisine
11. Pantry / Cellier
12. Storage / Rangements

13. Study / Bureau
14. Master bedroom / Chambre principale
15. Master bathroom / Salle de bains principale
16. Dressing room / Dressing
17. Gym / Salle de gym
18. Art room / Galerie d'art

Elevations / Élévations

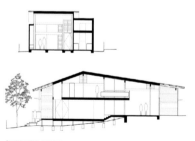

Sections / Vue en coupe

PADDINGTON X2 HOUSE

MCK Architecture & Interiors
Paddington, Sydney, NSW, Australia
© Willem Rethmeier

The transformation of two townhouses into one and the inclusion of sustainable passive elements represents a challenge for the architects. Efforts were focused on maintaining and reusing the original construction elements and achieving cross ventilation and effective insulation.

Die Verwandlung von zwei Reihenhäusern in ein einziges Wohngebäude und die Einbindung passiver Elemente zur Steigerung der Nachhaltigkeit stellten eine große Herausforderung an die Architekten. Man zielte darauf ab, die ursprünglichen Bauelemente zu erhalten und eine effiziente Kreuzlüftung und Isolierung zu erzielen.

La transformation de deux maisons mitoyennes en une, associée à l'incorporation d'éléments passifs compatibles avec le développement durable, représentait un défi pour les architectes. Leurs efforts ont porté sur le maintien et le réemploi des éléments existant, tout en créant une ventilation croisée et en produisant une isolation vraiment efficace.

De samenvoeging van twee geschakelde huizen tot één en de aanwending van passieve duurzaamheidselementen vormden een uitdaging voor de architecten. Hun inspanningen waren gericht op het handhaven en hergebruiken van de originele bouwelementen en om efficiënte kruisventilatie en isolatie te verkrijgen.

La transformación de dos casas adosadas en una y la inclusión de elementos pasivos de sostenibilidad supuso un reto para los arquitectos. Los esfuerzos se centraron en mantener y reutilizar los elementos constructivos originales y en conseguir una ventilación cruzada y un aislamiento realmente eficaces.

La trasformazione di due case adiacenti in un'unica struttura e l'inserimento di elementi passivi di sostenibilità hanno costituito una sfida per gli architetti. Si è mirato a preservare e riutilizzare gli elementi costruttivi originari e ottenere una ventilazione incrociata e un isolamento veramente efficaci.

A transformação de duas casas geminadas em uma e a inclusão de elementos passivos de sustentabilidade representou um desafio para os arquitetos. Os esforços centraram-se na manutenção e reutilização dos elementos de construção originais e na obtenção de uma ventilação cruzada e de um isolamento realmente eficazes.

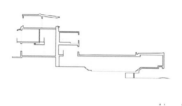

Sections / Vue en coupe

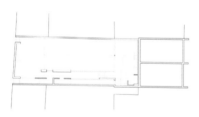

Ground floor / Rez-de-chaussée

Second floor / Premier étage

GAP HOUSE

Pitman Tozer Architects
Bayswater, London, UK
© Nick Kane

The challenge of the architects was to build a house with a low ecological footprint on a lot only 2.3 m (7.5 ft) wide. The use of glass and the open distribution towards the interior courtyard make the best use of light and the openings provide ventilation. The design means that the home only uses 30% of the energy that other similar homes use.

Die Architekten standen vor der Herausforderung, für ein lediglich 2,3 m breites Grundstück ein Haus mit möglichst kleinem ökologischen Fußabdruck zu planen. Durch die Verwendung von Glas und den zum Innenhof offenen Grundriss kann das Tageslicht voll ausgenutzt werden. Die Öffnungen sorgen außerdem für eine gute Belüftung. Dieses Gebäude verbraucht nur 30 % der Energie, die Wohnhäuser dieser Art üblicherweise konsumieren.

Les architectes ont relevé un défi consistant à construire une maison à empreinte écologique réduite sur une parcelle qui ne dépasse pas 2,3 m de large. L'usage du verre et la distribution ouverte sur le patio intérieur permettent de maximiser l'utilisation de la lumière ; les ouvertures assurent la ventilation. Grâce à sa conception, cette maison n'utilise que 30 % de l'énergie nécessaire à un logement de cette surface.

De uitdaging van de architecten was om een huis te bouwen met een kleine ecologische voetafdruk, op een perceel van slechts 2,3 m breed. Door het gebruik van glas en de open indeling naar de binnenplaats, kan het licht optimaal benut worden; de openingen zorgen voor ventilatie. Dankzij het ontwerp is het energieverbruik slechts 30% van het verbruik van woningen van hetzelfde type.

El reto de los arquitectos era construir una casa con una huella ecológica reducida en una parcela de solo 2,3 m de ancho. El uso del cristal y la distribución abierta hacia el patio interior aprovechan al máximo la luz, y las aberturas proporcionan ventilación. El diseño permite usar solo el 30% de la energía que utilizan las residencias de este tipo.

La sfida degli architetti era costruire una casa con un'impronta ecologica ridotta in un lotto di terreno di appena 2,3 di larghezza. L'uso del vetro e la distribuzione aperta verso il cortile interno consentono di sfruttare al massimo la luce; le aperture garantiscono la ventilazione. Il progetto consente di utilizzare appena il 30% dell'energia solitamente necessaria alle abitazioni di questo tipo.

O desafio dos arquitetos era construir uma casa com uma pegada ecológica reduzida numa parcela com apenas 2,3 m de largura. O uso do vidro e a distribuição aberta para o pátio interior aproveitam ao máximo a luz; as aberturas proporcionam ventilação. O design permite usar apenas 30% da energia utilizadas pelas habitações deste tipo.

Ground floor / Rez-de-chaussée

Second floor / Premier étage

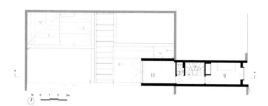

Third floor / Deuxième étage

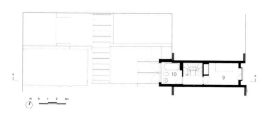

Fourth floor / Troisième étage

1. Entrance / Entrée
2. Heat pump / Local chaudière
3. Toilet / Sanitaires
4. Kitchen / Cuisine
5. Dining room / Salle à manger
6. Living room / Salon
7. Patio / Patio
8. Study / Bureau
9. Bedroom / Chambre
10. Bathroom / Salle de bains
11. Solarium / Solarium

NIEUW LEYDEN HOUSES

24H Architecture
Nieuw Leyden, The Netherlands
© Boris Zeisser 24H

These two homes have been built in a densely populated area and in narrow lots, which limit the entry of light. Central spaces that serve as circulation chimneys for air and that allow the entry of light were designed to promote natural lighting and cross ventilation. The wood used is certified.

Diese beiden Häuser wurden in einem dicht besiedelten Viertel auf sehr schmalen Grundstücken errichtet, die den Einfall von Tageslicht behindern. Um eine natürliche Beleuchtung und eine Kreuzlüftung zu erreichen, wurden kleine Lichthöfe in den Bau integriert, die Luftstrom und Tageslichteinfall verbessern. Die verwendeten Hölzer sind zertifiziert.

Ces deux logements ont été construits dans une zone de population dense sur des parcelles étroites, ce qui limite la pénétration de la lumière. Pour favoriser l'éclairage naturel et la ventilation croisée à l'intérieur, la distribution des pièces s'organise autour des espaces centraux qui tiennent lieu de puits de jour, permettant la circulation de l'air et l'entrée de la lumière. Le bois utilisé bénéficie d'une certification écologique.

Deze twee woningen zijn gebouwd in een dichtbevolkt gebied, op een aantal smalle percelen met weinig lichtinval. Om zo goed mogelijk gebruik te kunnen maken van hemellicht en kruisventilatie in het interieur zijn een aantal centrale ruimtes ontworpen die dienst doen als schoorstenen voor luchtcirculatie en lichtinval. Het gebruikte hout is voorzien van een certificaat.

Estas dos viviendas se han construido en una zona densamente poblada y en unas parcelas estrechas, que limitan la entrada de luz. Para favorecer la iluminación natural y la ventilación cruzada en los interiores se diseñaron unos espacios centrales que funcionan como chimeneas de circulación de aire y entrada de luz. La madera utilizada es certificada.

Queste due abitazioni sono state costruite in una zona densamente popolata e su lotti stretti che limitano l'ingresso della luce. Per favorire l'illuminazione naturale e la ventilazione incrociata negli ambienti interni, sono stati progettati degli spazi centrali che fungono da camini per il ricircolo di aria e l'ingresso di luce. Il legno utilizzato è di tipo certificato.

Estas duas casas foram construídas numa zona densamente povoada e em parcelas estreitas, que limitam a entrada de luz. Para favorecer a iluminação natural e a ventilação cruzada nos interiores foram projectados espaços centrais que funcionam como chaminés de circulação de ar e entrada de luz. A madeira utilizada é certificada.

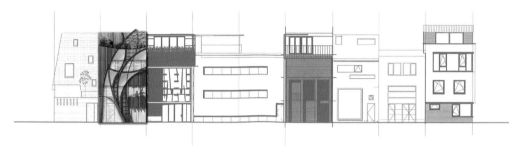

Voltastraat street elevation / Élévation de la rue Voltastraat

Wattstraat street elevation / Élévation de la rue Wattstraat

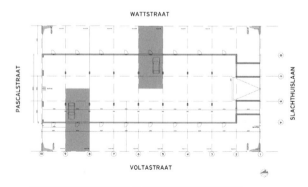

Location plan of the house in the block / Plan de situation dans le pâté de maisons

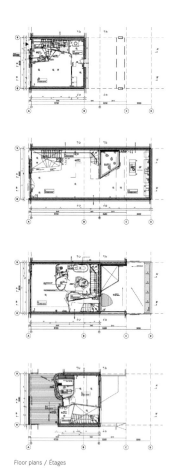

Floor plans / Étages

Elevations / Élévations

Sections / Vue en coupe

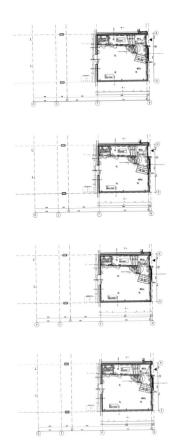

Floor plans / Étages

Elevations / Élévations

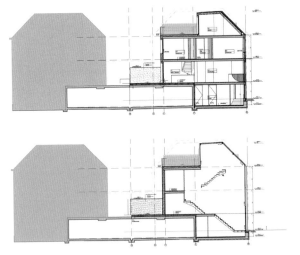

Sections / Vue en coupe

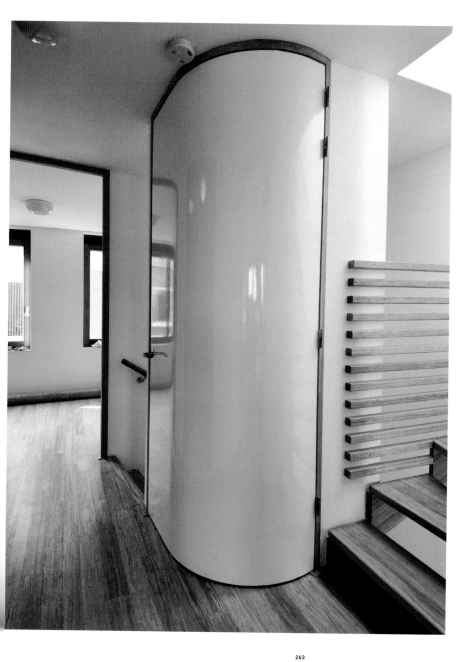

HOUSE AT HILLSIDE

Nota Design International
Singapore, Singapore
© Nota Design International

The refurbishment of this home in Singapore is focused on a more rational use of space and reducing the use of air conditioning as much as possible. The cross ventilation generated between the two façades and the vegetation of the courtyard cool the atmosphere naturally, and ceiling fans consume less power than conventional air conditioning.

Der Umbau dieses Hauses in Singapur sollte eine rationalere Raumnutzung und eine größtmögliche Reduzierung der Nutzung der Klimaanlage bewirken. Die Kreuzlüftung zwischen den beiden Fassaden und die Vegetation im Hof kühlen die Luft auf natürliche Weise, und Deckenventilatoren verbrauchen weniger Energie als herkömmliche Klimaanlagen.

Il s'agissait, en rénovant cette maison qui se situe à Singapour, de rationaliser l'exploitation de l'espace tout en réduisant au maximum l'usage de la climatisation. La ventilation croisée générée entre les deux façades et la végétation du patio rafraîchissent naturellement l'atmosphère. Les ventilateurs au plafond consomment moins qu'une climatisation conventionnelle.

De renovatie van deze in Singapore gelegen woning was gericht op het rationeler maken van de ruimte en om het gebruik van airconditioning tot een minimum te beperken. De kruisventilatie die tussen de twee gevels teweeg wordt gebracht en de vegetatie van de binnenplaats verfrissen de ruimte op natuurlijke wijze en de plafondventilatoren zijn zuiniger dan conventionele airconditioning.

La reforma de esta residencia de Singapur se centró en hacer más racional el espacio y en reducir lo máximo posible el uso del aire acondicionado. La ventilación cruzada que se genera entre las dos fachadas y la vegetación del patio refrescan el ambiente de forma natural, y los ventiladores del techo consumen menos que el aire acondicionado convencional.

La ristrutturazione di questa residenza di Singapore si è concentrata sulla razionalizzazione degli spazi e sulla riduzione dell'uso dell'aria condizionata nella misura del possibile. La ventilazione incrociata che si produce tra le due facciate e la vegetazione del cortile rinfrescano l'ambiente in modo naturale e i ventilatori sul soffitto consumano meno dell'aria condizionata standard.

A reforma desta habitação de Singapura centrou-se em tornar mais racional o espaço e em reduzir ao máximo o uso do ar condicionado. A ventilação cruzada gerada entre as duas fachadas e a vegetação do pátio refrescam o ambiente de forma natural, e os ventiladores do tecto consumem menos que o ar condicionado convencional.

Section / Vue en coupe

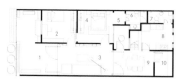

Ground floor / Rez-de-chaussée

Second floor / Premier étage

1. Patio / Patio
2. Bedroom / Chambre
3. Living room / Salon
4. Master bedroom / Chambre principale
5. Dressing room / Dressing
6. Ensuite / Salle de bains attenante

7. Bathroom / Salle de bains
8. Kitchen / Cuisine
9. Dining room / Salle à manger
10. Storage / Rangements
11. Study / Bureau

GOLD COAST BEACH HOUSE

BDA Architecture
Gold Coast, QLD, Australia
© Scott Burrows / Aperture Architectural Photography

The design of this home is carried out in order to take advantage of the breeze in the area. All façades have windows to generate cross ventilation; on the north and west façades shutters have been fitted that regulate the entry of sunshine in winter and summer. Furthermore, a rainwater collection tank allows it to be reused.

Beim Design dieses Hauses wurde das Ziel verfolgt, die dort herrschenden Winde maximal auszunutzen. Sämtliche Fassaden wurden mit Fenstern versehen, um eine Kreuzlüftung zu ermöglichen. An der Nord- und Westfassade wurden Jalousien angebracht, welche die Regulierung der einfallenden Sonnenstrahlen im Sommer und Winter ermöglichen. Ein Auffangtank ermöglicht die Wiederverwendung des Regenwassers.

La conception des plans de cette maison visait à tirer un parti maximum des vents de la zone. Tous les murs ont des fenêtres afin de générer une ventilation croisée. Sur les façades nord et ouest, les persiennes permettent la régulation de l'entrée du soleil hiver comme été. De plus, un réservoir recueille les eaux pluviales qui sont donc utilisées.

Het ontwerp van dit huis is gemaakt met als doel om de wind van het gebied zo goed mogelijk te benutten. Alle gevels hebben ramen om kruisventilatie mogelijk te maken en aan de noord- en westgevel zijn zonneblinden bevestigd waarmee de inval van zonlicht in de winter en in de zomer kan worden geregeld. Bovendien kan met een regenwatertank het hemelwater worden hergebruikt.

El diseño de esta casa se realizó con el objetivo de aprovechar al máximo las brisas de la zona. Todas las fachadas tienen ventanas para generar ventilación cruzada, y en las fachadas norte y oeste se han instalado persianas que regulan la entrada de sol en invierno y en verano. Además, un tanque de recogida de aguas pluviales permite reutilizar el agua de la lluvia.

Questa casa è stata realizzata con l'obiettivo di sfruttare al massimo le brezze della zona. Tutte le facciate dispongono di finestre per produrre ventilazione incrociata e sulle facciate nord e ovest sono state aggiunte delle persiane che regolano l'ingresso del sole in inverno e in estate. Inoltre, un serbatoio consente di raccogliere e riutilizzare l'acqua piovana.

O projecto desta casa foi concebido com o objectivo de aproveitar ao máximo as brisas da zona. Todas as fachadas têm janelas para gerar ventilação cruzada, e nas fachadas norte e oeste foram instaladas persianas que regulam a entrada de sol no Inverno e no Verão. Adicionalmente, um tanque de recolha de águas pluviais permite reutilizar a água da chuva.

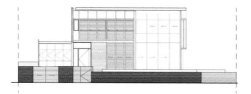

North elevation / Élévation nord

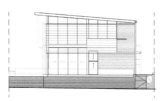

West elevation / Élévation ouest

Section / Vue en coupe

Ground floor / Rez-de-chaussée

Second floor / Premier étage

MONA VALE HOUSE

Choi Ropiha
Mona Vale, NSW, Australia
© Simon Whitbread, Brett Boardman

The Sustainable Energy Development Agency (SEDA) and the architects have designed a home with different sustainability strategies: photovoltaic panels, hydronic radiant floor heating, a 15,000 liter (3,960 gal) tank to collect rainwater and another to recycle graywater.

Die Zusammenarbeit zwischen der Energieagentur für nachhaltige Energieentwicklung (SEDA) und den Architekten haben den Entwurf dieses Wohnhauses ermöglicht, das mit unterschiedlichen Nachhaltigkeitsstrategien aufwartet: es verfügt über Photovoltaikpaneele, eine Warmwasser-Fußbodenheizung, einen Regenwassertank mit einer Kapazität von 15.000 Litern und einen weiteren Tank für die Wiederverwendung von Grauwasser.

La collaboration entre l'Agence pour le Développement d'Énergie Soutenable (SEDA) et les architectes a permis de concevoir une demeure alliant plusieurs stratégies de développement durable : des panneaux solaires photovoltaïques, un chauffage par plancher radiant hydronique, un réservoir d'une capacité de 15 000 litres pour recueillir l'eau de pluie et un second pour le recyclage des eaux grises.

De samenwerking tussen de Ontwikkelingsautoriteit voor Duurzame Energie (SEDA) en de architecten heeft het mogelijk gemaakt om een woning te ontwerpen met verschillende strategieën door de duurzaamheid: fotovoltaïsche zonnepanelen, vloerverwarming met straling, een tank met een inhoud van 15.000 liter voor het opvangen van regenwater en een voor hergebruik van grijs water.

La colaboración entre la Agencia de Desarrollo de Energía Sostenible (SEDA) y los arquitectos ha permitido diseñar una residencia con diferentes estrategias para la sostenibilidad: paneles solares fotovoltaicos, calefacción de suelo radiante hidrónico, un tanque con capacidad de 15.000 litros para recoger el agua de lluvia y otro para reciclar las aguas grises.

La collaborazione tra SEDA (Agenzia sviluppo energia sostenibile) e gli architetti ha consentito di progettare un'abitazione con diverse strategie per la sostenibilità: pannelli solari fotovoltaici, riscaldamento a pavimento radiante idronico, un serbatoio con 15.000 litri di capacità per la raccolta dell'acqua piovana e un altro per il riciclo delle acque grigie.

A colaboração entre a Agência de Desenvolvimento de Energia Sustentável (SEDA) e os arquitectos permitiu projectar uma casa com diferentes estratégias para a sustentabilidade: painéis solares fotovoltaicos, aquecimento de piso radiante hidrónico, um tanque com capacidade de 15.000 litros para recolha de água da chuva e outro para reciclar as águas cinzentas.

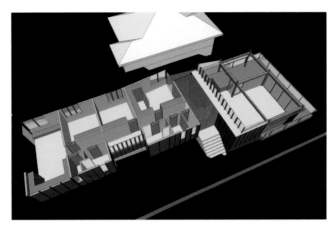

Axonometric view / Vue axonométrique

East elevation / Élévation est

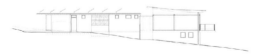

West elevation / Élévation ouest

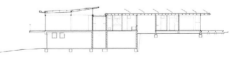

Longitudinal section / Coupe longitudinale

Plan / Étage

1. Entrance / Entrée
2. Dining room / Salle à manger
3. Living room / Salon
4. Kitchen / Cuisine

5. Bathroom / Salle de bains
6. Bedroom / Chambre
7. Laundry / Buanderie
8. Solarium / Solarium

Site plan / Plan de situation

Green features diagram / Croquis des installations écologiques

PIEDRA ROJA

Riesco + Rivera Arquitectos Asociados
Santiago, Chile
© Sebastián Wilson León, www.swl.cl

If natural resources are utilized, and the design and orientation are correct, you can reduce the energy consumption of air conditioning. The longest façade has a north-south orientation, which favors the sun in winter and shade in summer. The location of the patios and the windows allow for cross ventilation and the stack effect.

Wenn natürliche Ressourcen genutzt werden und Design und Ausrichtung gut durchdacht sind, kann der Energieverbrauch für die Klimatisierung gesenkt werden. Die längste Fassade mit Nord-Süd-Ausrichtung nutzt im Winter die Sonne und im Sommer den Schatten. Die Anordnung der Innenhöfe und Fenster ermöglicht die Kreuzlüftung und den Kamineffekt.

Quand on exploite les ressources naturelles, si le plan et l'orientation sont judicieux, la consommation d'énergie liée à la climatisation baisse de façon spectaculaire. La façade la plus longue est exposée nord-sud, favorisant le soleil en hiver et l'ombre en été. L'emplacement des patios et des fenêtres permet une ventilation croisée et l'effet cheminée.

Als de natuurlijke hulpbronnen worden benut en het ontwerp en de oriëntatie goed zijn, kan het energieverbruik voor luchtbehandeling worden teruggedrongen. De langste gevel heeft een oriëntatie noord-zuid, waardoor de zon in de winter naar binnen kan schijnen en er in de zomer schaduw wordt geboden. De ligging van de patio's en de ramen maken kruisventilatie en een schoorsteeneffect mogelijk.

Si se aprovechan los recursos naturales, y el diseño y la orientación son buenos, se puede reducir el consumo energético derivado de la climatización. La fachada más larga tiene una orientación norte-sur, lo que favorece el sol en invierno y la sombra en verano. La ubicación de los patios y de las ventanas permite una ventilación cruzada y el efecto chimenea.

Se si sfruttano le risorse naturali e il progetto e l'orientamento sono buoni, è possibile ridurre il consumo di energia derivato dalla climatizzazione. La facciata più lunga ha un orientamento nord-sud; ciò favorisce il sole in inverno e l'ombra in estate. L'ubicazione dei cortili e delle finestre consente una ventilazione incrociata e il cosiddetto effetto camino.

Caso se aproveitem os recursos naturais, e se a concepção e a orientação são correctas, pode reduzir-se o consumo energético derivado da climatização. A fachada mais longa tem uma orientação norte-sul, o que favorece o sol no Inverno e a sombra no Verão. A localização dos pátios e das janelas permite uma ventilação cruzada e o efeito chaminé.

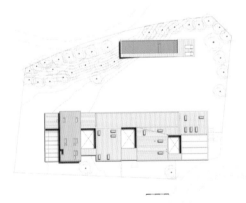

Location plan / Plan de situation

Elevations / Élévations

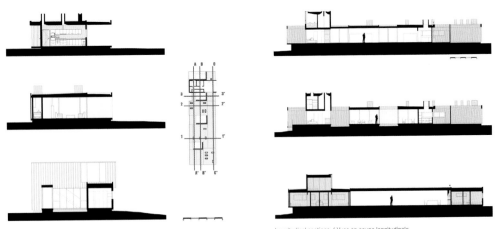

Cross sections / Vues en coupe transversale

Longitudinal sections / Vues en coupe longitudinale

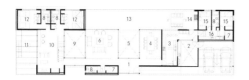

Ground floor / Rez-de-chaussée

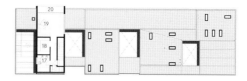

Second floor / Premier étage

1. Hall / Hall d'entrée
2. Working patio / Patio de travail
3. Kitchen / Cuisine
4. Dining room / Salle à manger
5. Patio / Patio
6. Living room / Salon
7. Storage / Rangements

8. Bathroom / Salle de bains
9. Green patio / Patio vert
10. Family room / Séjour
11. Playground patio / Patio de jeux
12. Bedroom / Chambre
13. Corridor / Couloir
14. Barbecue / Barbecue

15. Service rooms / Chambres de service
16. Laundry / Buanderie
17. Master bathroom / Salle de bains principale
18. Dressing room / Dressing
19. Master bedroom / Chambre principale
20. Balcony / Balcon

CROWSNEST MODULAR HOME

Conquest Manufacturing
Crowsnest Pass, AB, Canada
© Lori Andrews

The owners wanted a house open to the landscape that is energy efficient, zero maintenance and minimal environmental impact. The orientation of the house and the modular construction with insulation materials meet the objectives, such as a 30% reduction in energy consumption.

Die Eigentümer wünschten sich ein zur umgebenden Landschaft hin offenes Haus, das mit einer hohen Energieeffizienz, geringstmöglichem Wartungsaufwand und minimalen Umweltwirkungen aufwartet. Die Ausrichtung des Hauses und der modulare Bau mit dämmenden Materialien erfüllen die gesteckten Ziele und führten zu einer Reduzierung des Energieverbrauchs um 30 %.

Les propriétaires souhaitaient une maison ouverte sur le paysage, d'une grande efficacité énergétique, dont l'impact sur l'environnement serait nul ou minime. L'orientation du logement et la construction modulaire avec des matériaux isolants permettent d'atteindre ces objectifs, avec une réduction de 30 % de la consommation en énergie.

De eigenaars wilden een huis dat open stond naar het landschap, met een grote energetische efficiëntie, dat onderhoudsvrij was en met een minimale impact op het milieu. De oriëntatie van de woning en de modulaire constructie met isolerende materialen voldoen aan de doelstellingen, met 30% minder energieverbruik.

Los propietarios deseaban una casa abierta al paisaje, de gran eficiencia energética, mantenimiento nulo y mínimo impacto medioambiental. La orientación de la vivienda y la construcción modular con materiales aislantes cumplen con los objetivos, como una reducción del 30% del consumo energético.

I proprietari desideravano avere una casa aperta sul paesaggio, ad alta efficienza energetica, con manutenzione nulla e minimo impatto ambientale. L'orientamento dell'abitazione e la costruzione modulare con materiali isolanti raggiungono questi obiettivi, tra cui la riduzione del 30% dei consumi energetici.

Os proprietários pretendiam uma casa aberta à paisagem, de grande eficiência energética, sem manutenção e com impacto ambiental mínimo. A orientação da casa e a construção modular com materiais isolantes cumprem esses objectivos, permitindo uma redução de 30% do consumo energético.

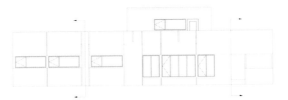

Front elevation / Élévation frontale

Left elevation / Élévation gauche

Right elevation / Élévation droite

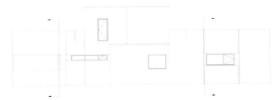

Back elevation / Élévation postérieure

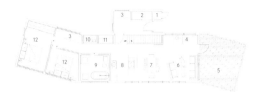

Ground floor / Rez-de-chaussée

Second floor / Premier étage

1. Seasonal storage / Rangements d'été
2. Bicycle storage / Rangements à vélos
3. Window seating / Banc pour admirer le panorama
4. Woodstove / Poêle à biomasse
5. Covered deck / Terrasse couverte
6. Living room / Salon
7. Dining room / Salle à manger

8. Kitchen / Cuisine
9. Bathroom / Salle de bains
10. Washroom and laundry / Buanderie
11. Closet / Armoire
12. Bedroom / Chambre
13. Study / Bureau
14. Terrace / Terrasse

PUTNEY MOUNTAIN HOUSE

Kyu Sung Woo Architects
Putney, VT, USA
© Kyu Sung Woo Architects

This located on the southeast face of the Putney Mountains is completely off-the-grid. This energy self-sufficiency is achieved through photovoltaic panels. The thick walls insulate the interior from temperature changes and a biomass boiler heats the water with wood collected in the forest.

Dieses Wohnhaus am Südwesthang des Putney Mountain verfügt über keinerlei Anbindung an das Stromnetz. Diese Energieautarkie wird mithilfe von Photovoltaikpaneelen erzielt. Dicke Mauern schirmen das Innere von den außen herrschenden Temperaturunterschieden ab und ein Biomasseofen erwärmt das Haus mit im Wald gesammeltem Brennholz.

Cette maison, sur le versant sud-ouest de la montagne Putney, n'est pas raccordée au réseau électrique. Les panneaux photovoltaïques assurent son autonomie en énergie. Ses murs épais isolent l'intérieur, le protégeant des variations de température et un poêle à biomasse chauffe la maison avec le bois coupé dans la forêt.

Deze woning, gelegen op de zuidwestelijke helling van de berg Putney, is helemaal afgesloten van het lichtnet. De energetische zelfvoorziening is mogelijk dankzij fotovoltaïsche panelen. De dikke muren isoleren het interieur tegen temperatuurschommelingen en een biomassakachel verwamt het huis met in het bos verzameld hout.

Esta residencia, situada en la ladera sudoeste de la montaña Putney, está completamente desconectada de la red eléctrica. Esta autosuficiencia energética se consigue gracias a paneles fotovoltaicos. Las gruesas paredes aíslan el interior de los cambios de temperatura y una estufa de biomasa calienta la casa con madera recogida en el bosque.

Questa casa, situata sulle pendici sudovest del monte Putney, è totalmente staccata dalla rete di fornitura elettrica. Tale autosufficienza energetica si ottiene grazie all'uso di pannelli fotovoltaici. Le spesse pareti isolano gli ambienti interni dai cambiamenti di temperatura e una stufa a biomassa riscalda la casa con il legname raccolto nel bosco.

Esta casa, situada na encosta sudoeste da montanha Putney, está completamente desligada da rede elétrica. Esta auto-suficiência energética é conseguida graças a painéis fotovoltaicos. As paredes espessas isolam o interior das mudanças de temperatura e um fogão de sala biomassa aquece a casa com madeira recolhida na floresta.

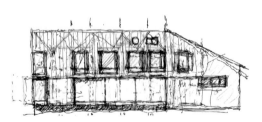

Sketches / Croquis

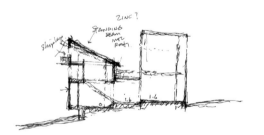

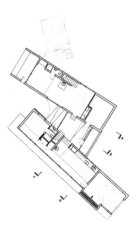

Floor plan / Étage

EMU BAY HOUSE

Max Pritchard Architect
Kangaroo Island, SA, Australia
© Sam Noonan

In this summer house energy saving passive strategies have been used such as window insulation and the distribution of openings, which create ventilation to cool down the interior, with others such as the collection and storage of rainwater. The corrosion-resistant galvanized steel tanks stand out.

Bei diesem Sommerhaus wurden passive Energiesparmaßnahmen umgesetzt, wie z. B. eine gute Isolierung der Fenster und eine durchdachte Anordnung der Fassadenöffnungen, die für eine kühlende Belüftung des Inneren sorgt. Des Weiteren wurde ein Regenwasserauffangsystem installiert. Besonders hervorzuheben sind die korrosionsbeständigen Verkleidungen aus feuerverzinktem Stahl.

Pour cette résidence d'été, on a fait appel aux stratégies passives d'économie d'énergie, comme l'isolation des fenêtres et la distribution des ouvertures – qui génèrent la ventilation nécessaire pour rafraîchir l'intérieur – ou la collecte et le stockage de l'eau de pluie. On remarque les réservoirs en acier galvanisé conçus pour résister à la corrosion.

In dit zomerverblijf is rekening gehouden met passieve strategieën voor energiebesparing, zoals de isolatie van de ramen en de indeling van de openingen –die zorgen voor ventilatie om het binnen koel te houden–, en andere strategieën zoals het opvangen en opslaan van regenwater. Opvallend zijn de roestwerende tanks van gegalvaliseerd staal.

En esta residencia de verano se han tenido en cuenta estrategias pasivas de ahorro energético, como el aislamiento de las ventanas y la distribución de las aberturas –que generan ventilación para refrescar el interior–, con otras como la recogida y el almacenamiento de agua de lluvia. Destacan los tanques de acero galvanizado, resistente a la corrosión.

In questa casa per le vacanze estive sono state applicate le strategie passive di risparmio energetico come l'isolamento delle finestre e la distribuzione delle aperture che generano ventilazione per rinfrescare gli ambienti interni, oltre alla raccolta e alla conservazione dell'acqua piovana. Si notino i serbatoi in acciaio galvanizzato, resistente alla corrosione.

Nesta casa de Verão foram tidas em conta estratégias passivas de poupança energética, como o isolamento das janelas e a distribuição das aberturas, as quais geram ventilação para refrescar o interior, e outras como a recolha e o armazenamento de água da chuva. Os tanques de aço galvanizado resistente à corrosão ganham especial destaque.

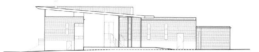

West elevation / Élévation ouest

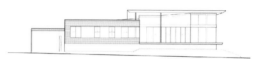

East elevation / Élévation est

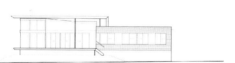

North elevation / Élévation nord

South elevation / Élévation sud

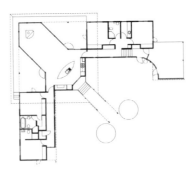

Plan / Étage

THE FLOAT HOUSE

Morphosis Architects in association with UCLA Architecture and Urban Design,
for Make It Right
New Orleans, LA, USA
© Iwan Baan

In addition to a prefabricated design that saves costs and CO_2 emissions, the house designed
for those affected by hurricane Katrina includes solar panels that provide electricity and a roof
that collects rainwater that is then filtered and reused. The geothermal heating completes the
environmental measures.

Neben einem vorgefertigten Design, das Kosten spart und den CO_2-Ausstoß senkt, weist dieses
für Opfer des Hurrikans Katrina entworfene Haus Sonnenkollektoren für die Stromerzeugung
und ein speziell geformtes Dach auf, welches Regenwasser für die anschließende Filterung
und Wiederverwertung auffängt. Eine weitere umweltschonende Maßnahme ist die integrierte
Erdwärmeheizung.

En dehors de sa conception préfabriquée, qui fait baisser les coûts et les émissions de CO_2, cette
maison conçue pour les victimes de l'ouragan Katrina produit son électricité grâce à ses panneaux
solaires. La forme de la toiture permet la récupération des eaux de pluie qui sont filtrées avant d'être
utilisées. Le chauffage géothermique complète l'ensemble des mesures environnementales.

Naast een ontwerp met voorgefabriceerde elementen, waardoor kosten worden bespaard en de
CO_2-uitstoot wordt verminderd, is het huis, ontworpen voor de benadeelden van de orkaan Karina,
voorzien van zonnepanelen die elektriciteit leveren en een dak dat een zodanige vorm heeft dat
het regenwater wordt opgevangen, dat vervolgens wordt gefilterd en kan worden hergebruikt. De
geothermische verwarming maakt het geheel van milieuvriendelijke maatregelen compleet.

Además de un diseño prefabricado que ahorra costes y emisiones de CO_2, la casa, concebida para
los afectados por el huracán Katrina, incluye placas solares, que proporcionan electricidad. La
forma del tejado permite recoger el agua de la lluvia para su filtrado y reutilización. La calefacción
geotérmica completa el conjunto de medidas medioambientales.

Oltre all'idea del prefabbricato che riduce costi ed emissioni di CO_2, la casa, realizzata per gli sfollati
dell'uragano Katrina, comprende pannelli solari per la produzione di elettricità e un tetto la cui
forma consente di raccogliere l'acqua piovana che poi viene filtrata e riutilizzata. Il riscaldamento
geotermico completa l'insieme delle misure a favore dell'ambiente.

Além de uma concepção pré-fabricada que poupa custos e emissões de CO_2, a casa, concebida
para as pessoas atingidas pelo furacão Katrina, inclui painéis solares, que proporcionam
electricidade, e um telhado com uma forma que recolhe a água da chuva para posterior filtragem e
reutilização. O aquecimento geotérmico completa o conjunto de medidas ambientais.

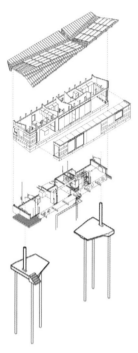

Diagram of the main features of the house / Croquis des éléments principaux de la maison

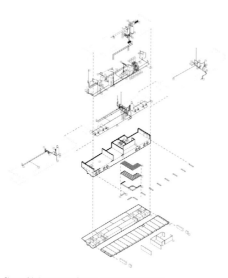

Diagram of the house chassis / Croquis du soubassement de la maison

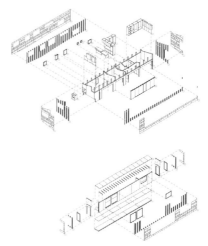

Diagram of wall system / Croquis des revêtements

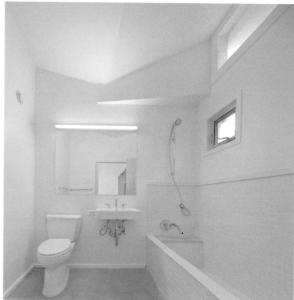

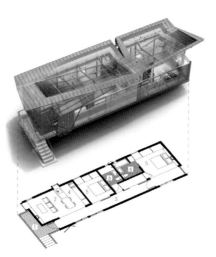

Axonometric view and floor plan / Axonométrie et étage

1. Porch / Porche
2. Living room / Salon
3. Gallery / Galerie
4. Kitchen / Cuisine
5. Bedroom / Chambre
6. Bathroom / Salle de bains

SANTA MONICA PREFAB

Office of Mobile design by Jennifer Siegal
Santa Monica, CA, USA
© Laura Hull

This prefabricated house saves on costs and CO_2 emissions. The paints are free of volatile organic compounds (VOCs) and the adhesives are non-toxic. Significant use was made of recycled materials, such as the aluminum in exterior doors and windows, and of insulating materials like low-e glass, which keeps heat in winter and prevents heat from entering in summer.

Dieses Fertighaus spart Kosten und verringert den CO_2-Ausstoß. Die verwendeten Farben sind frei von VOCs, die ausgewählten Klebstoffe sind vollkommen ungiftig. Hervorzuheben sind die recycelbaren Materialien wie das Aluminium der Außentüren und Fenster, sowie Dämmstoffe wie Low-E-Fenster, die im Winter wie im Sommer für ein gutes Raumklima sorgen.

Cette maison préfabriquée est économe et génère un minimum de CO_2. Les peintures ne contiennent pas de composés organiques volatils et les adhésifs ne renferment aucun composant toxique. On remarque les matériaux recyclables, comme l'aluminium des portes extérieures et des fenêtres, ou isolant, comme le verre à basse émissivité, qui conserve la chaleur en hiver et l'empêche de pénétrer en été.

Bij dit geprefabriceerde huis worden kosten bespaard en wordt de CO_2-uitstoot verminderd. De verf bevat geen vluchtige organische stoffen en de hechtmiddelen hebben geen giftige bestanddelen. Opvallend zijn de recyclebare materialen zoals het aluminium van de buitendeuren en de ramen, of isolatiemateriaal, zoals *low-e*-glas, dat in de winter de warmte binnenhoudt en in de zomer voorkomt dat het binnendringt.

Esta casa prefabricada ahorra costes y emisiones de CO_2. Las pinturas no contienen compuestos orgánicos volátiles y los adhesivos no poseen componentes tóxicos. Destacan los materiales reciclables, como el aluminio de las puertas exteriores y las ventanas, o aislantes, como el cristal *low-e*, que mantiene el calor en invierno y evita que penetre en verano.

Questa casa prefabbricata consente di ridurre spese ed emissioni di CO_2. Le vernici non contengono composti organici volatili e i collanti non contengono sostanze tossiche. Si impongono i materiali riciclabili come l'alluminio delle porte esterne e le finestre, o quelli isolanti come il vetro a basso emissivo che mantiene il calore in inverno e ne evita l'ingresso in estate.

Esta casa pré-fabricada reduz os custos e as emissões de CO_2. As tintas não contêm compostos orgânicos voláteis e as colas não possuem componentes tóxicos. Destacam-se os materiais recicláveis, como o alumínio das portas exteriores e das janelas, ou os isolantes, como o vidro *low-e*, que mantém o calor no Inverno e evita a entrada deste no Verão.

Ground floor / Rez-de-chaussée

Second floor / Premier étage

1. Entrance / Entrée
2. Kitchen / Cuisine
3. Living – dining room / Salon – Salle à manger
4. Chimney / Cheminée
5. Garage / Garage
6. Bathroom / Sanitaires
7. Laundry room / Buanderie

8. Mechanical room / Pièce technique
9. Storage / Rangements
10. Bedroom / Chambre
11. Bathroom / Salle de bains
12. Study / Bureau
13. Main bathroom / Salle de bains principale
14. Main bedroom / Chambre principale

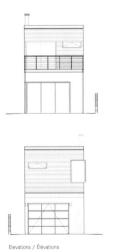

Elevations / Élévations

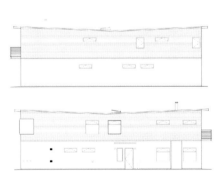

SAFE HOUSE

Robert Konieczny
Warsaw, Poland
© KWK PROMES

The original mechanical openings of this home mean that the home can follow the day/night transition. Conventional energy resources coexist with solar panels and the openings that promote cross ventilation and natural lighting is combined with thick walls and strategies that retain the heat generated throughout the day.

Die originellen mechanischen Fassadenöffnungen dieses Wohnhauses sorgen dafür, dass die Bauweise dem Tag-Nacht-Zyklus folgt. Herkömmliche Energieressourcen wurden mit Sonnenkollektoren kombiniert, die Fenster begünstigen die Kreuzlüftung und der Tageslichteinfall wurde optimiert. Außerdem wurden dicke Mauern errichtet und Strategien umgesetzt, die die erzeugte Wärme den Tag über aufrechterhalten.

Les ouvertures mécaniques inhabituelles de cette maison lui permettent de suivre le cycle des jours et des nuits. Les énergies conventionnelles complètent la production des panneaux solaires. Les ouvertures favorisent la ventilation croisée et l'éclairage naturel. Elles s'associent aux murs épais et aux stratégies permettant de conserver la chaleur produite durant la journée.

Dankzij de originele mechanische openingen van deze woning kan in de architectuur de dag- en nachtcyclus worden gevolgd. Conventionele energetische hulpbronnen worden gecombineerd met zonnepanelen en de openingen maken kruisventilatie en natuurlijke licht mogelijk. De dikke muren en andere strategieën houden de warmte die gedurende de dag is gegenereerd vast.

Las originales aberturas mecánicas de esta residencia logran que la arquitectura siga el ciclo de día y noche. Los recursos energéticos convencionales conviven con placas solares y las aberturas que favorecen la ventilación cruzada y la iluminación natural se combinan con gruesas paredes y estrategias que mantienen el calor generado durante el día.

Le originali aperture meccaniche di questa abitazione fanno sì che l'architettura segua il ciclo del giorno e della notte. Le risorse energetiche convenzionali convivono con pannelli solari mentre le aperture che favoriscono la ventilazione incrociata e l'illuminazione naturale si combinano a spesse pareti e a strategie che mantengono il calore generato durante il giorno.

As originais aberturas mecânicas desta casa conseguem que a arquitetura siga o ciclo de dia e noite. Os recursos energéticos convencionais convivem com placas solares e as aberturas que favorecem a ventilação cruzada e a iluminação natural são combinadas com paredes espessas e estratégias que preservam o calor gerado durante o dia.

North-east elevations / Élévations nord-est

South-west elevations / Élévations sud-est

South-east elevations / Élévations sud-ouest

North-west elevations / Élévations nord-ouest

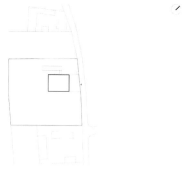

Site plan / Plan de situation

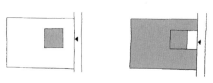

Open and closed house diagram / Croquis de la maison ouverte et fermée

Cross section / Coupe transversale

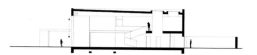

Longitudinal section / Coupe longitudinale

Ground floor open and closed house plan / Rez-de-chaussée ouvert et fermé

Second floor open and closed house plan / Premier étage ouvert et fermé

BUDAPEST XVI

Zsuffa és Kalmár Építész Műterem
Budapest, Hungary
© Tamás Bujnovszky

Although it seems obvious, sustainable architecture begins with awareness on the best possible use of the characteristics of the land and the orientation of the buildings. It is about trying to adapt the house to the environment without losing character. On this occasion, the orientation, insulation and the use of local materials achieve major energy savings.

Es mag vielen offensichtlich erscheinen: Die nachhaltige Architektur beginnt mit der Bewusstmachung, wie bestimmte Standortmerkmale und die Ausrichtung der Gebäude genutzt werden können. Es geht darum, sich vorzustellen, wie das Haus an die Umgebung angepasst werden kann, ohne dass es gleichzeitig seinen eigenen Charakter verliert. In diesem Beispiel konnte durch eine optimale Ausrichtung, Isolierung und die Verwendung lokaler Materialien eine große Energieersparnis erzielt werden.

C'est une évidence : l'architecture durable commence par la prise de conscience de la nécessité d'utiliser les caractéristiques du terrain et l'orientation des constructions. Il faut imaginer comment adapter la maison à son environnement tout en conservant son caractère. Pour ce chantier, l'orientation, l'isolation et l'usage de matériaux locaux ont permis de réaliser d'importantes économies d'énergie.

Hoewel het logisch lijkt, begint de duurzame architectuur met de bewustwording over de benutting van de kenmerken van het terrein en de oriëntatie van de bouwwerken. Er wordt daarbij getracht om een voorstelling te maken van hoe het huis kan worden aangepast aan de omgeving, zonder dat het aan karakter inboet. In dit geval wordt door oriëntatie, isolatie en het gebruik van plaatselijke materialen veel energie bespaard.

Aunque parezca obvio, la arquitectura sostenible comienza con la concienciación sobre el aprovechamiento de las características del terreno y la orientación de las construcciones. Se trata de imaginar cómo adaptar la casa al entorno sin que pierda su personalidad. En esta ocasión, la orientación, el aislamiento y el uso de materiales locales consiguen un gran ahorro energético.

Anche se pare ovvio, l'architettura sostenibile parte dall'uso attento delle caratteristiche del terreno e l'orientamento degli edifici. Si tratta di immaginare come adattare la casa al contesto circostante senza che perda carattere. In questo caso l'orientamento, l'isolamento e l'uso di materiali locali consentono un importante risparmio energetico.

Embora pareça óbvio, a arquitetura sustentável começa com a tomada de consciência sobre o aproveitamento das características do terreno e a orientação das construções. Trata-se de imaginar como adaptar a casa ao ambiente circundante sem que perca personalidade. Neste contexto, a orientação, o isolamento e o uso de materiais locais conseguem assegurar uma grande poupança energética.

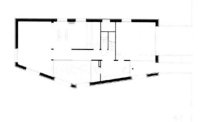

Ground floor / Rez-de-chaussée

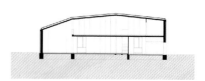

Section / Vue en coupe

Second floor / Premier étage

Sketch / Croquis

HOUSE O

Andrea Tognon Architecture
Teolo, Italy
© Andrea Tognon

The most common problem in old houses is the lack of insulation. The refurbishment of this home has solved the wastefulness of energy and lack of comfort. The Styrodur panels and insulated windows and frames mean that the warmth generated by the new heating system, from solar panels, remains on the interior.

Das häufigste Problem bei alten Häusern besteht in der mangelnden Isolierung. Beim Umbau dieses Wohnhauses wurde der Energieverschwendung Einhalt geboten und der Komfort wurde erhöht. Die Styrodur-Platten, die Fenster und die wärmedämmenden Fenster- und Türrahmen halten die mithilfe des neuen Heizsystems über Sonnenkollektoren erzeugte Wärme im Inneren des Hauses.

Le problème le plus fréquent dans les maisons anciennes est l'absence d'isolation. La réhabilitation de ce logement a résolu la perte considérable d'énergie et le manque de confort. Grâce aux panneaux Styrodur, aux fenêtres et aux huisseries isolantes, la chaleur générée par le nouveau système de chauffage, provenant de panneaux solaires, reste à l'intérieur.

Het meest voorkomende probleem bij oude huizen is een gebrekkige isolatie. Het opknappen van deze woning heeft de energieverspilling en het gebrek aan comfort opgelost. De Styrodur panelen en de ramen met isolerende kozijnen maken het mogelijk dat de gegenereerde warmte door de nieuwe verwarming, afkomstig van de zonnepanelen, binnen blijft.

El problema más frecuente de las casas antiguas es la falta de aislamiento. La rehabilitación de esta vivienda ha solucionado el derroche de energía y la falta de confort. Los paneles Styrodur y las ventanas y los marcos aislantes permiten que el calor generado por la nueva calefacción, procedente de placas solares, se quede en el interior.

Il problema più frequente delle case vecchie è la mancanza di isolamento. La ristrutturazione di questa abitazione ha risolto lo spreco di energia e lo scarso comfort. I pannelli di Styrodur e le finestre con cornici isolanti fanno sì che il calore generato dal nuovo sistema di riscaldamento - ottenuto tramite pannelli solari - resti all'interno.

O problema mais frequente das casas antigas é a falta de isolamento. A recuperação desta habitação solucionou o desperdício de energia e a falta de conforto. Os painéis Styrodur, as janelas e os caixilhos isolantes permitem que o calor gerado pelo novo aquecimento, proveniente de painéis solares, permaneça no interior.

Section/ Vue en coupe

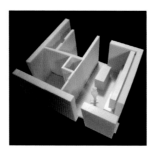

Model / Maquette

3D rendering / Représentation en 3D

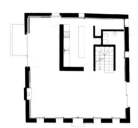

Ground floor / Rez-de-chaussée

Second floor / Premier étage

GLIDEHOUSE

Michelle Kaufmann Studio
Novato, CA, USA
© John Swain

The designs by Michelle Kaufmann perfectly comply with the task of building with sustainable techniques and materials using advanced assembly systems. Materials such as certified low VOC adhesives and varnishes have been used. The air-conditioning is carried out with a heat exchanger.

Die Entwürfe von Michelle Kaufmann erfüllen dank fortschrittlicher Montagesysteme die Prämisse des Bauens unter Einsatz nachhaltiger Materialien und Verfahren. Bei diesem Haus wurden zertifizierte Hölzer sowie Klebstoffe und Lacke mit einem niedrigen Gehalt an VOCs verwendet. Die Klimatisierung erfolgt über einen Wärmetauscher.

Les plans de Michelle Kaufmann réalisent à la perfection la mission de construire avec des matériaux et des techniques respectueuses de l'environnement en utilisant des systèmes d'assemblages avancés. On a veillé à n'utiliser que des bois certifiés, adhésifs et vernis contenant très peu de composés organiques volatils. La climatisation est assurée par un échangeur de chaleur.

De ontwerpen van Michelle Kaufmann voldoen tot in de finesses aan de missie van het bouwen met duurzame materialen en technieken door middel van geavanceerde montagesystemen. Er is gebruik gemaakt van materialen zoals gecertificeerd hout en van hechtmiddelen en lakken met een laag gehalte aan vluchtige organische stoffen. De luchtbehandeling is mogelijk met een warmtewisselaar.

Los diseños de Michelle Kaufmann cumplen a la perfección la misión de construir con materiales y técnicas sostenibles mediante sistemas de ensamblaje avanzados. Se han utilizado materiales como madera certificada y adhesivos y barnices con una bajo contenido de compuestos orgánicos volátiles. La climatización se realiza con un intercambiador de calor.

I progetti di Michelle Kaufmann soddisfano pienamente l'obiettivo di costruire utilizzando materiali e tecniche sostenibili tramite sistemi di assemblaggio avanzati. Sono stati utilizzati materiali come il legno certificato e collanti e vernici a basso contenuto di composti organici volatili. La climatizzazione avviene tramite uno scambiatore di calore.

Os projectos de Michelle Kaufmann cumprem na perfeição a missão de construir com materiais e técnicas sustentáveis através de sistemas de montagem avançados. Foram utilizados materiais como madeira certificada e colas e vernizes com um baixo conteúdo de compostos orgânicos voláteis. A climatização é realizada através de um permutador de calor.

355

Factory production / Production industrielle

On site button up / Montage sur site

Completed Glidehouse / Glidehouse achevée

a.   Roof structure / Structure de la toiture
b.   Hidden up-lighting / Éclairage (au sol) vers le haut dissimulé
c.   Clerestory windows / Rangée de lanterneaux
d.   Storage bar / Barre de rangements
e.   Siding glass wall / Parois de verre coulissante
f.   Site installed solar panels / Panneaux solaires assemblés sur site
g.   Site installed standing seam metal roofing / Toiture métallique assemblée sur site
h.   Roof brackets / Support de la toiture
i.   Siding wood screens / Panneaux – Cloisons coulissantes en bois
j.   Site built foundation / Fondations
k.   Site built deck / Plate-forme fabriquée sur site

Main floor / Niveau principal

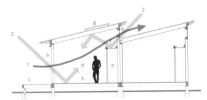

Bioclimatic diagram / Diagramme bioclimatique

a. Siding-glass-door wall / Porte coulissante en verre
b. Clerestory windows / Rangée de lanterneaux
c. Outdoor room / Pièce à ciel ouvert
d. Indoor living / Séjour intérieur
e. Storage bar with customizable shelving behind
    sliding wooden doors / Barre de rangements avec
    étagères modulables dissimulées par des portes
    coulissantes en bois
f. Up-lighting / Éclairage bas dirigé vers le haut

g. Solar panels on metal standing-seam roofing /
    Panneaux solaires sur toiture métallique
h. Bamboo flooring / Parquet en bambou
i. Energy-efficient insulation / Isolant très performant
1. Cross ventilation in all the main spaces /
    Ventilation croisée dans toutes les grandes pièces
2. Balanced daylighting-indirect lighting / Équilibre
    entre la lumière du jour et l'éclairage indirect

VERMONT CABIN

Resolution: 4 Architecture
Jamaica, VT, USA
© Resolution: 4 Architecture

Prefabricated homes, a specialty of this studio, are a less invasive form of architecture on the environment. Here a concrete base has been built on which the modules are placed. Other sustainable elements are the photovoltaic solar panels and recyclable and natural wood such as the bamboo used in the floor and the cedar used on the exterior.

Fertighäuser greifen weniger in die Natur ein als andere Bauweisen. Hier wurde ein Betonfundament errichtet, auf dem die einzelnen Module installiert wurden. Weitere nachhaltige Elemente sind Photovoltaikpaneele sowie recycelte und natürliche Hölzer, wie z. B. beim Fußboden aus Bambus und der Außenverkleidung aus Zedernholz.

Las habitations préfabriquées, spécialité de ce cabinet d'architectes, signifient une architecture moins invasive pour le milieu ambiant. Ici, on a coulé une dalle de béton sur laquelle on a ensuite placé les modules. Les autres éléments respectueux de l'environnement sont les panneaux solaires photovoltaïques et les bois recyclés et naturels, comme le bambou des sols et le cèdre à l'extérieur.

Geprefabriceerde woningen, de specialiteit van deze studio, zijn onderdeel van een milieuvriendelijkere architectuur. Hier is een betonnen ondergrond aangelegd, waarop de modules zijn geplaatst. Andere duurzame elementen zijn de fotovoltaïsche zonnepanelen en recyclebaar en natuurlijk hout, zoals de bamboe vloer en het gebruik van cederhout buiten.

Las viviendas prefabricadas, la especialidad de este estudio, suponen una arquitectura menos invasiva con el medio ambiente. Aquí se ha construido una base de hormigón sobre la que se colocan los módulos. Otros elementos sostenibles son las placas solares fotovoltaicas y maderas reciclables y naturales, como el bambú del suelo y el cedro exterior.

Le abitazioni prefabbricate, soluzione in cui è specializzato questo studio, riflettono un'architettura meno invasiva nei confronti dell'ambiente. In questo caso è stata realizzata una base di cemento sulla quale vengono poi sistemati i moduli. Altri elementi sostenibili sono i pannelli solari fotovoltaici e il legno riciclabile e naturale come il bambù applicato sul pavimento e il cedro all'esterno.

As habitações pré-fabricadas, a especialidade deste estúdio, implicam uma arquitetura menos invasiva para com o ambiente. Aqui, foi construída uma base de betão sobre a qual foram colocados os módulos. Outros elementos sustentáveis são os painéis solares fotovoltaicos e as madeiras recicláveis e naturais, como o bambu do chão e o cedro exterior.

Floor plan / Rez-de-chaussée

1. Entrance / Entrée
2. Laundry room / Buanderie
3. Kitchen / Cuisine
4. Dining room / Salle à manger
5. Living room / Salon

6. Media room / Salle multimédia
7. Bathroom / Salle de bains
8. Bedroom / Chambre
9. Main bathroom / Salle de bains principale
10. Main bedroom / Chambre principale

GIDGEGANNUP RESIDENCE

Iredale Pedersen Hook Architects
Gidgegannup, WA, Australia
© Andrew Pritchard, Patrick Bingham-Hall

Several measures of sustainability are included in this home: an elevated construction for minimal impact on the natural environment, high insulation in the windows and in the floor to prevent energy loss, origin-controlled wood and materials that require little maintenance and rainwater collection for reuse.

Bei diesem Wohnhaus wurden mehrere Nachhaltigkeitsmaßnahmen umgesetzt: eine erhöhte Bauweise für eine minimale Beeinträchtigung der natürlichen Umgebung, eine effektive Fenster- und Fußbodendämmung zur Vermeidung von Energieverlusten, Hölzer aus kontrollierter Forstwirtschaft, wartungsarme Materialien und ein Regenwasserauffangsystem für diverse Einsatzgebiete.

Plusieurs mesures en faveur du développement durable ont été mises en place dans cette demeure, qui a été édifiée avec le souci d'avoir un impact minimum sur son environnement naturel. Elle est très bien isolée grâce au vitrage et à un sol conçus pour limiter les déperditions d'énergie. Le bois est certifié provenant de forêts gérées et les matériaux employés demandent peu d'entretien. Les eaux de pluie sont récupérées pour différents usages.

In deze woning zijn verschillende maatregelen van duurzaamheid genomen: een verhoogde constructie met een minimale impact op de natuurlijke omgeving, een grote mate van isolatie in de ramen en de vloer om verlies van energie te voorkomen, hout van gecontroleerde oorsprong en onderhoudsvriendelijk materiaal en de opvang van regenwater dat op verschillende manieren weer kan worden gebruikt.

Esta residencia cuenta con varias medidas de sostenibilidad: una construcción elevada para un mínimo impacto en el entorno natural, un gran aislamiento en los cristales y en el suelo para evitar pérdidas de energía, maderas de origen controlado o materiales que requieren poco mantenimiento y recogida de agua de lluvia para su reutilización en diferentes usos.

Questa abitazione applica varie misure di sostenibilità: una costruzione sopraelevata per causare il minimo impatto sull'ambiente naturale, un grande isolamento tramite i vetri e il pavimento al fine di evitare la dissipazione di energia, l'uso di legname di origine controllata o materiali che richiedono scarsa manutenzione e la raccolta di acqua piovana che viene poi riutilizzata in vari modi.

Nesta residência estão incluídas várias medidas de sustentabilidade: uma construção elevada para um impacto mínimo no meio natural, um grande isolamento nos vidros e no solo para evitar perdas de energia, madeiras de origem controlada ou materiais que requerem pouca manutenção e recolha de água da chuva para posterior reutilização em diferentes aplicações.

North-east elevation / Élévation nord-est

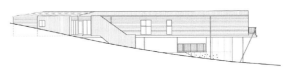

South elevation / Élévation sud

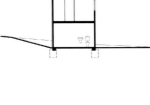

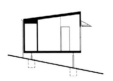

Sections / Vue en coupe

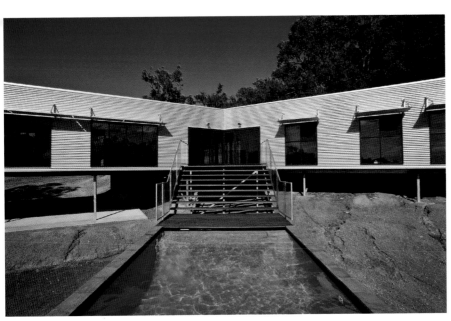

Ground floor / Rez-de-chaussée

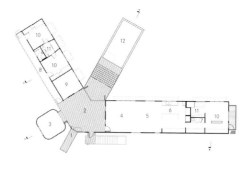

Second floor / Premier étage

1. Dining-living room / Salon - salle à manger
2. Kitchen / Cuisine
3. Study / Bureau
4. Master bedroom / Chambre principale
5. Bathroom / Salle de bains
6. Garage / Garage
7. Outdoor dining / Salon extérieur
8. Green roof / Couverture végétale
9. Living room / Salle de séjour
10. Bedroom / Chambre
11. Laundry / Buanderie
12. Mechanical room / Pièce technique

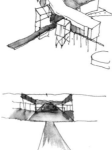

Sketches / Croquis

LAVAFLOW 3

Craig Steely Architecture
Big Island, HI, USA
© Cesar Rubio

The positioning on pillars so as to not alter the natural setting and the orientation of the house and its openings are the strongholds of this architect. The use of air currents that can be modified through the use of blinds and curtains make air-conditioning unnecessary. The rainwater is stored and reused.

Der Architekt dieses Hauses bewies mit dem Bau auf Stelzen zur Verringerung der Geländebelastung und der Ausrichtung von Haus und Fassadenöffnungen viel Geschick. Die Ausnutzung der Luftströme, die mithilfe von Jalousien und Vorhängen reguliert werden können, machen eine Klimaanlage überflüssig. Das Regenwasser wird aufgefangen und wiederverwendet.

Respectueuse du terrain, la construction sur pilotis ainsi que l'orientation de la maison et des ouvertures sont les plus belles réussites de l'architecte sur ce projet. La domestication des flux d'air, sur lesquels on agit via les persiennes et les rideaux, dispense d'installer une climatisation. L'eau de pluie est récupérée afin d'être utilisée.

De ligging op pilaren om de natuurlijke omgeving in stand te houden en de oriëntatie van het huis en de openingen zijn de beste beslissingen van deze architect. De benutting van de luchtstromen, die dankzij zonneblinden en gordijnen kunnen worden gewijzigd, maakt airconditioning overbodig. Het regenwater wordt opgeslagen en hergebruikt.

La situación sobre pilares para no alterar el terreno natural y la orientación de la casa y de sus aberturas son los mejores aciertos de este arquitecto. El aprovechamiento de las corrientes de aire, que pueden modificarse gracias a persianas y cortinas, hace innecesario el aire acondicionado. El agua de la lluvia se almacena y se reutiliza.

Il posizionamento della struttura sopra dei pilastri per non alterare il terreno naturale e l'orientamento della casa e delle sue aperture rappresentano le scelte vincenti di questo architetto. Lo sfruttamento delle correnti d'aria, che possono essere modificate tramite persiane e tende, rende inutile un impianto di condizionamento. L'acqua piovana viene raccolta per essere poi riutilizzata.

O posicionamento sobre pilares para não alterar o terreno natural e a orientação da casa e das suas aberturas foram as melhores opções deste arquitecto. O aproveitamento das correntes de ar, que podem ser modificadas graças às persianas e cortinas, torna desnecessário o ar condicionado. A água da chuva é armazenada e reutilizada.

Location plan / Plan de situation

Floor plan / Rez-de-chaussée

CABIN VARDEHAUGEN

Fantastic Norway Architects
Åfjord, Norway
© Fantastic Norway Architects

For the design of this house, the wind in the region had to be studied, which was carried out with the help of the locals and the thesis by Anne Britt Børve on the design of buildings in cold locations. The positioning of the volumes creates small terraces protected from the wind. The biomass boiler and triple glazed windows retain heat in the interior.

Beim Entwurf dieses Hauses untersuchte man die regionalen Winde mithilfe von Einheimischen und einer Doktorarbeit über das Design von Gebäuden an kalten Standorten. Durch die Anordnung der Baukörper entstehen kleine windgeschützte Terrassen. Der Biomasseofen und die Dreifachverglasung halten die Wärme im Inneren aufrecht.

En préliminaire au dessin des plans, on a réalisé une étude des vents de cette zone d'après les informations fournies par la population locale et en se référant à la thèse de Anne Britt Børve sur la réalisation de bâtiment dans les régions froides. L'agencement des volumes crée de petites terrasses protégées des vents. Le poêle à biomasse et le triple vitrage des fenêtres conservent la chaleur à l'intérieur.

Voor het ontwerp van dit huis was een bestudering van de wind in de zone onontbeerlijk. Dit is gedaan met behulp van de plaatselijke bewoners en het proefschrift van Anne Britt Børve over het ontwerp van gebouwen in koude streken. De oriëntatie van de woongedeeltes creëert kleine terrassen in de luwte. De biomassakachel en het driedubbele glas in de ramen houden de warmte in het interieur vast.

Para el diseño de esta casa se partió de un estudio de los vientos de la zona, realizado a raíz de las informaciones proporcionadas por los habitantes, y de la tesis de Anne Britt Børve sobre la arquitectura en lugares fríos. La distribución de los volúmenes crea pequeñas terrazas protegidas del viento. La estufa de biomasa y triple vidrio en las ventanas mantienen el calor del interior.

Per la progettazione di questa casa è stato fondamentale studiare i venti della zona con l'aiuto degli abitanti del luogo e utilizzando i dati della tesi di Anne Britt Børve sulla progettazione di edifici in luoghi freddi. La particolare posizione dei volumi dà vita a piccoli ambienti esterni protetti dal vento. La stufa a biomassa e i tripli vetri alle finestre mantengono il calore negli ambienti interni.

Para a concepção desta casa foi indispensável o estudo dos ventos da zona, realizado com a ajuda da população local e da tese de Anne Britt Børve sobre a concepção de edifícios em locais frios. O posicionamento dos volumes cria pequenos terraços protegidos do vento. O recuperador de biomassa e o vidro triplo nas janelas mantêm o calor no interior.

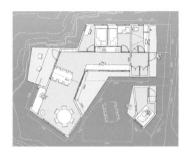

Floor plan / Rez-de-chaussée

Sections / Vues en coupe

REMODELED FARMHOUSE

Jeffrey McKean Architect
Claryville, NY, USA
© Keith Mendenhall, Jeffrey McKean Architect

The remodeling of this farmhouse was used to include better sustainable criteria. The new volume uses the glue-lam wooden structure and insulating panels. The cedar certified wood used for the siding and the glass panes are highly insulated and are positioned to facilitate cross ventilation.

Im Rahmen der Renovierung des Bauernhauses wurde die Gelegenheit genutzt, um einen Anbau zu errichten, der diverse Nachhaltigkeitskriterien erfüllt. Der neue Baukörper besteht aus einer Struktur aus Brettschichtholz mit Dämmplatten. Für die Verkleidung wurde zertifiziertes Zedernholz verwendet. Die Fenster mit hohem Dämmwert wurden so angeordnet, dass eine Kreuzlüftung ermöglicht wird.

La surélévation de la grange a permis la réalisation d'une extension conforme aux critères du développement durable. La structure de ce nouveau volume est en bois *gluelam* et est composée de panneaux isolants. Le revêtement est en cèdre provenant de forêts gérées ; les vitrages présentent un haut niveau d'isolation. L'emplacement des fenêtres facilite la ventilation croisée.

De renovatie van de boerderij werd benut voor een uitbouw met duurzame criteria. Het nieuwe gedeelte gebruikt een *glue-lam* houten structuur en isolerende panelen. De bekleding is van gecertificeerd cederhout en de ramen hebben een grote mate van isolatie en zijn zo geplaatst dat er kruisventilatie kan plaatsvinden.

La rehabilitación de la granja se aprovechó para realizar una ampliación de criterios sostenibles. El nuevo volumen tiene una estructura de madera *glue-lam* y paneles aislantes. El revestimiento es de madera certificada de cedro y los cristales presentan un elevado grado de aislamiento y una ubicación que facilita la ventilación cruzada.

La ristrutturazione di questa fattoria è stata l'occasione per realizzare un ampliamento applicando i criteri di sostenibilità. Il nuovo volume utilizza una struttura di legno *glue-lam* e pannelli isolanti. Il rivestimento è in legno certificato di cedro mentre i vetri hanno un elevato livello di isolamento e sono posizionati in modo da facilitare la ventilazione incrociata.

A recuperação da casa da quinta foi aproveitada para realizar uma ampliação de critérios sustentáveis. O novo volume utiliza estrutura de madeira *glue-lam* e painéis isolantes. O revestimento é de madeira certificada de cedro e os vidros apresentam um elevado nível de isolamento e uma localização que facilita a ventilação cruzada.

Site plan / Plan de situation

North elevation / Élévation nord

East elevation / Élévation est

South elevation / Élévation sud

West elevation / Élévation ouest

Longitudinal section / Coupe longitudinale

Cross section / Coupe transversale

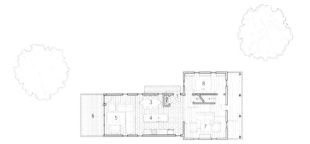

Ground floor / Rez-de-chaussée

Second floor / Premier étage

1. Entrance / Entrée
2. Closet / Armoire
3. Dining room / Salle à manger
4. Kitchen / Cuisine
5. Living room / Salon

6. Terrace / Terrasse
7. Family room / Salle de séjour
8. Study / Bureau
9. Bedroom / Chambre
10. Bathroom / Salle de bains

LEBLANC HOUSE

Peter Cardew Architects
West Vancouver, BC, Canada
© Peter Cardew, Sarah Murray

The energy savings in a home is the first step to sustainability. Therefore, insulation should be optimal. The refurbishment of this home has achieved improved thermal insulation through the installation of more efficient windows. The use of local materials and respect for the architecture of the area are outstanding elements.

Eine Steigerung der Energieersparnis ist der erste Schritt zu mehr Nachhaltigkeit. Daher muss ein Wohnhaus optimal isoliert werden. Beim Umbau dieses Hauses konnte die Wärmedämmung durch energieeffiziente Fenster verbessert werden. Die Verwendung lokaler Materialien und der Respekt vor der regionalen Bauweise sind ebenfalls hervorzuheben.

Les économies d'énergie dans une demeure sont le premier pas vers un développement durable. C'est pourquoi l'isolation doit être très performante. La rénovation a consisté à améliorer l'isolation en installant des fenêtres plus efficaces. La préférence accordée aux matériaux locaux et le respect de l'architecture régionale rendent ce travail remarquable.

Energiebesparing in een woning is de eerste stap in de richting van duurzaamheid. De isolatie moet daarom optimaal zijn. Met de renovatie van deze woning is men erin geslaagd om de warmte-isolatie te verbeteren door middel van de installatie van efficiëntere ramen. Het gebruik van plaatselijke materialen en het respecteren van de streekarchitectuur zijn andere opvallende elementen.

El ahorro de energía en una residencia es el primer paso para ganar en sostenibilidad. Por lo tanto, el aislamiento debe ser óptimo. La reforma de esta vivienda ha conseguido una mejora del aislamiento térmico mediante la instalación de ventanas más eficientes. El uso de materiales locales y el respeto por la arquitectura de la zona son otros elementos destacables.

Il risparmio energetico in una casa rappresenta il primo passo verso la sostenibilità. Quindi l'isolamento deve essere ottimale. La ristrutturazione di questa abitazione ha consentito di ottenere un miglioramento dell'isolamento termico tramite l'installazione di finestre con un'efficienza maggiore. L'uso di materiali locali e il rispetto per l'architettura della zona sono altri elementi importanti.

A poupança de energia numa residência é o primeiro passo para ganhar em sustentabilidade. Portanto, o isolamento deve ser óptimo. A reforma desta habitação permitiu uma melhoria do isolamento térmico através da instalação de janelas mais eficientes. O uso de materiais locais e o respeito pela arquitectura da zona são outros elementos a destacar.

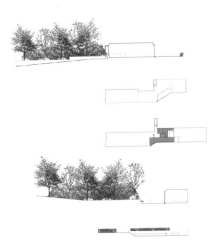

Sections / Vues en coupe

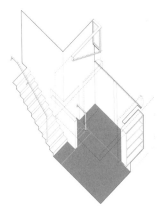

Stair diagram / Diagramme de l'escalier

Before – after floor plans / Plan des étages avant et après

Ground floor and second floor (new configuration) / Redistribution des étages

LES-GWEN MCDONALD HOUSE

Martin Liefhebber/Breathe Architects
Prince Edward County, ON, Canada
© Martin Liefhebber

This house, completely self-sufficient in terms of energy, includes apart from thermal and photovoltaic panels, a wind turbine and solar kitchen. Likewise, the thermal mass from the concrete floor is used and the north walls have been insulated with bales of hay. The thermal break of the doors and windows improve the insulation of the interior.

Dieses vollkommen energieautarke Haus ist mit Wärmekollektoren, Photovoltaikpaneelen, einer Windkraftanlage und einem Solarkocher ausgestattet. Ferner nutzt man die Wärmespeicherung im Betonboden. Die Nordwand wurde mit Strohballen isoliert. Durch Türen und Fenster mit thermischer Trennung wird die Wärmedämmung der Innenräume verbessert.

Outre les panneaux solaires thermiques et photovoltaïques, cette maison, entièrement autonome en énergie, dispose d'une éolienne et d'une cuisine solaire. Elle bénéficie également de la masse thermique d'un soubassement de béton ; le mur nord a été isolé avec des bottes de paille. La rupture des ponts thermiques des portes et fenêtres améliore l'isolation.

Dit voor wat betreft de energie volledig zelfvoorzienende huis heeft naast thermische en fotovoltaïsche zonnepanelen een windgenerator en een zonnekooktoestel. Bovendien wordt gebruik gemaakt van thermische massa van een betonnen plaat en is de muur aan de noordzijde geïsoleerd met strobalen. De koudebrugonderbreking van de deuren en ramen zorgt voor een betere isolatie binnen.

Esta casa, completamente autosuficiente en cuanto a energía, incluye, además de placas solares térmicas y fotovoltaicas, un generador eólico y una cocina solar. Asimismo, se aprovecha la masa térmica de un solado de hormigón y se ha aislado el muro norte con balas de paja. La rotura del puente térmico de puertas y ventanas aísla mejor el interior.

Questa casa, completamente autosufficiente in termini energetici, dispone oltre che di pannelli solari termici e fotovoltaici di un generatore eolico e di una cucina solare. Inoltre viene sfruttata la massa termica del solaio di cemento e la parete nord è stata isolata con balle di paglia. La rottura del ponte termico di porte e finestre isola meglio gli ambienti interni.

Esta casa, completamente auto-suficiente quanto a energia, inclui, para além de painéis solares térmicos e fotovoltaicos, um gerador eólico e um fogão solar. De igual modo, é aproveitada a massa térmica de um chão de betão e isolou-se a parede norte com fardos de palha. A ruptura da ponte térmica de portas e janelas isola melhor o interior.

Elevation / Élévation

Floor plan / Rez-de-chaussée

A. Thermal mass wall / Mur de masse thermique
B. Solar kitchen / Cuisine solaire
C. Straw bales wall / Mur en bottes de paille
1. Entrance / Entrée
2. Laundry room / Buanderie
3. Kitchen / Cuisine
4. Living room / Salon
5. Outdoor living / Salon extérieur
6. Bathroom / Salle de bains
7. Dressing room / Dressing
8. Bedroom / Chambre
9. Garage / Garage

DALKEITH RESIDENCE

Iredale Pedersen Hook Architects
Perth, WA, Australia
© Iredale Pedersen Hook Architects

The aesthetics of green homes have changed. This elegant home saves water and energy with low-flow valve, low-energy lights and cross ventilation, but it also has thermal and photovoltaic solar panels and rain collection tanks. The choice of low impact ecological footprint materials completes the sustainable measures.

Das Aussehen von Öko-Häusern hat sich gewandelt. Dieses elegante Wohnhaus spart Wasser und Strom mithilfe von Durchflussbegrenzern, Energiesparlampen und Kreuzlüftung und wurde außerdem mit Photovoltaikpaneelen, Wärmekollektoren und Regenwassertanks ausgestattet. Eine weitere Maßnahme für mehr Nachhaltigkeit war die Nutzung von Materialien mit möglichst kleinem ökologischen Fußabdruck.

L'esthétique des maisons écologiques a changé. Cet élégant logement économise l'eau, avec une robinetterie munie de réducteur de pression, et l'énergie par l'emploi d'éclairages basse consommation et sa ventilation croisée. Il possède également des panneaux solaires thermiques et photovoltaïques et des réservoirs de récupération des eaux de pluie. Le choix de matériaux à faible empreinte écologique complète cette panoplie de mesures en faveur d'un développement durable.

De esthetiek van de ecologische huizen is veranderd. In deze elegante woning worden niet alleen water en energie bespaard door middel van debietregelaars, ledlampen en kruisventilatie, maar er is ook voorzien in thermische en fotovoltaïsche zonnepanelen en tanks voor de opvang van regenwater. De keuze voor materialen met een kleinere ecologische voetafdruk is de aanvulling op de duurzame maatregelen.

La estética de las casas ecológicas ha cambiado. Esta elegante vivienda ahorra agua y energía con reductores de caudal, luces de bajo consumo y ventilación cruzada, pero también posee paneles solares térmicos y fotovoltaicos y tanques de recolección de lluvia. La elección de materiales de menor huella ecológica completa las medidas sostenibles.

L'estetica delle case ecologiche è cambiata. Questa elegante abitazione risparmia acqua ed energia tramite riduttori di flusso, luci a basso consumo e ventilazione incrociata, ma dispone anche di pannelli solari termici e fotovoltaici oltre a serbatoi per la raccolta dell'acqua piovana. La scelta di materiali con una minore impronta ecologica completa questo approccio a favore della sostenibilità.

A estética das casas ecológicas mudou. Esta elegante casa poupa água e energia utilizando redutores de caudal, luzes de baixo consumo e ventilação cruzada, mas também possui painéis solares térmicos e fotovoltaicos e tanques para recolha de chuva. A escolha de materiais com menor pegada ecológica completa as medidas sustentáveis.

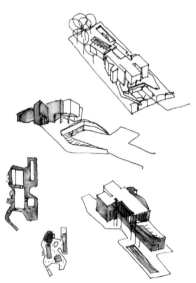

Sketches / Croquis

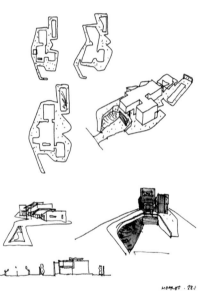

Ground floor / Rez-de-chaussée

Second floor / Premier étage

1. Entrance / Entrée
2. Living room / Salon
3. Dining room / Salle à manger
4. Kitchen / Cuisine
5. Lounge / *Lounge*
6. Outdoor living / Salon extérieur
7. Laundry / Buanderie
8. Cellar / Bar – Cave
9. Play room / Salle de jeux
10. Guest room / Chambre d'amis
11. Bathroom / Salle de bains
12. Storage – Workshop / Rangements – Atelier
13. Pool / Piscine
14. Studio / Bureau
15. Bedroom / Chambre
16. Closet / Armoire

BROOKS AVENUE HOUSE

Bricault Design
Venice, CA, USA
© Kenji Arai, Danna Kinsky

The new volume of this home, built as a second extension, stands out for its walls and green roof. Local plants have been used, therefore they require less maintenance. As well as for irrigation, rainwater is reused for domestic use. Low VOC paints and varnishes have been used as finishes.

Der im Rahmen eines zweiten Ausbaus errichtete neue Baukörper dieses Wohnhauses besticht durch seine Wände und das bepflanze Dach. Da es sich um einheimische Pflanzen handelt, fällt der erforderliche Pflegeaufwand geringer aus. Das gesammelte Regenwasser wird nicht nur zu Bewässerung, sondern auch im Haushalt wiederverwendet. Für die Oberflächenbearbeitung mit Farben und Lacken wurden Produkte mit niedrigem Gehalt an flüchtigen organischen Verbindungen ausgewählt.

Le nouveau volume de cette villa, avec ses murs et sa couverture végétale, constitue un second agrandissement qui ne passe pas inaperçu. Les plantes sont endémiques et demandent donc peu d'entretien. L'eau de la pluie sert à l'arrosage ainsi qu'à divers usages domestiques. Les peintures et vernis choisis pour les finitions contiennent peu de composés organiques volatils.

Het nieuwe gedeelte van deze woning, dat is gebouwd als tweede uitbouw, valt op door de met planten begroeide muren en dak. De planten zijn autochtoon waardoor ze weinig onderhoud nodig hebben. Behalve voor het besproeien wordt regenwater benut voor huishoudelijk gebruik. De afwerkingen zijn uitgevoerd met verf en lak met een laag gehalte aan vluchtige organische stoffen.

Construida como una segunda ampliación, el nuevo volumen de esta residencia destaca por las paredes y la cubierta vegetales. Las plantas son autóctonas, por lo que requieren menos mantenimiento. Además de para el riego, el agua de la lluvia se reutiliza para usos domésticos. Los acabados, como pinturas y barnices, son de bajo contenido en compuestos orgánicos volátiles.

Costruito come un secondo ampliamento, il nuovo volume di questo edificio si impone per le pareti e il rivestimento vegetale. Le piante sono autoctone e richiedono di conseguenza una minore manutenzione. Oltre che per irrigare, l'acqua piovana serve anche per uso domestico. Le finiture, come pitture e vernici, sono a basso contenuto di composti organici volatili.

Construído como uma segunda ampliação, o novo volume desta casa destaca-se pelas paredes e cobertura vegetais. As plantas são autóctones, pelo que requerem menos manutenção. A água da chuva, além de ser reutilizada para rega, também é utiliza em aplicações domésticas. Os acabamentos, como pinturas e vernizes, são de baixo teor em compostos orgânicos voláteis.

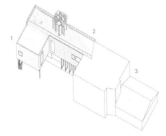

Axonometric / Axonométrie

1. New addition / Deuxième extension
2. Second addition (90's) / Premier agrandissement (années 1990)
3. Original cottage (40's) / Construction d'origine (années 1940)

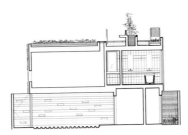

Sections / Vue en coupe

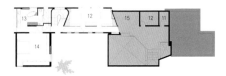

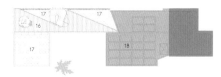

Floor plans / Étages

1. Mechanical room / Pièce technique
2. Laundry / Buanderie
3. Storage / Rangements
4. Patio / Patio
5. Hall / Receveur
6. Kitchen / Cuisine
7. Living room / Salon
8. Pantry / Cellier
9. Storage / Sanitaires

10. Powder / Toilette
11. Bathroom / Salle de bains
12. Bedroom / Chambre
13. Main bathroom / Salle de bains principale
14. Main bedroom / Chambre principale
15. Study / Bureau
16. Green roof / Couverture végétale
17. Vegetable garden / Jardin potager
18. Solar panels / Panneaux solaires

TALIESIN MOD.FAB

Taliesin Design/Build Studio, Office of Mobile Design by J. Siegal, M.P. Johnson
Design Studio
Scottsdale, AZ, USA
© Bill Timmerman

The prefabricated homes by Jennifer Siegal are already a reference in this type of architecture and great allies for environmental sustainability. The Structural Insulated Panels (SIP) reduce both the time and cost. In addition, the house can be connected to the grid or the energy can be obtained from solar panels, rainwater is also collected.

Die Fertighäuser von Jennifer Siegal haben sich im Bereich der umweltgerechten Architektur bereits einen Namen gemacht und stehen für ökologische Nachhaltigkeit. Die vorgefertigten SIP-Platten sorgen für eine Senkung der Bauzeit und der Kosten. Außerdem kann das Haus an das Stromnetz angebunden werden oder elektrische Energie über die Sonnenkollektoren erzeugen. Das Regenwasser wird aufgefangen und wiederverwendet.

Les résidences préfabriquées de Jennifer Siegal sont déjà une référence en matière de développement durable. Les panneaux isolants préfabriqués (SIP) réduisent la durée et les coûts des chantiers. De plus, la maison peut être raccordée au réseau électrique ou générer sa propre énergie grâce à ses panneaux solaires. Les eaux pluviales sont recueillies.

De voorgefabriceerde woningen van Jennifer Siegal zijn inmiddels uitgegroeid tot een referent op het gebied van dit soort architectuur en vormen grote bondgenoten voor het behalen van duurzaamheid. De voorgefabriceerde isolerende panelen (SIP) dragen bij aan tijd- en kostenbesparing. Bovendien kan het huis zowel worden aangesloten op het lichtnet als energie ontvangen van de zonnepanelen, en wordt er regenwater opgevangen.

Las residencias prefabricadas de Jennifer Siegal son ya un referente en este tipo de arquitectura y unas grandes aliadas de la sostenibilidad medioambiental. Los paneles aislantes prefabricados (SIP) reducen tiempo y costes. Además, la casa puede conectarse a la red u obtener energía de los paneles solares, y también recoge las aguas pluviales.

Le abitazioni prefabbricate di Jennifer Siegal sono già un punto di riferimento in questo tipo di architettura e grandi alleate della sostenibilità ambientale. I pannelli isolanti prefabbricati (SIP) riducono i tempi e i costi. Inoltre la casa può essere collegata alla fornitura elettrica tradizionale od ottenere energia dai pannelli solari e dispone di sistema per la raccolta dell'acqua piovana.

As casas pré-fabricadas de Jennifer Siegal são já uma referência neste tipo de arquitectura bem como grandes aliadas da sustentabilidade ambiental. Os painéis isolantes pré-fabricados (SIP) reduzem tempo e custos. Adicionalmente, a casa pode ser ligada à rede ou obter energia dos painéis solares, além de recolher também as águas pluviais.

West elevation / Élévation ouest

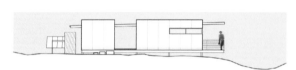

North elevation / Élévation nord

East elevation / Élévation est

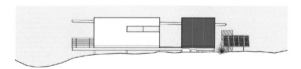

South elevation / Élévation sud

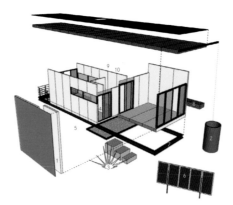

Diagram of the environmental features of the house / Croquis des installations écologiques de la maison

1. S.I.P. construction – floor, walls, roof / Panneaux isolants structurels SIP
2. Rainwater harvesting / Réservoir d'eaux pluviales
3. Grey water re-use for vegetation / Réemploi des eaux grises pour l'arrosage
4. Natural ventilation / Ventilation croisée
5. Solar orientation / Orientation

6. Photovoltaics / Panneaux photovoltaïques
7. Transportable structure / Structure transportable
8. Drought tolerant landscaping / Végétation supportant la sécheresse
9. On demand water heater / Chauffe-eau
10. Off the grid ability / Possibilité d'autonomie énergétique

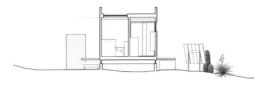

Cross section / Coupe transversale

Plan / Étage

Longitudinal section / Coupe longitudinale

1. Entrance / Entrée
2. Covered breezeway / Passerelle couverte
3. Bedroom / Chambre
4. Kitchen / Cuisine

5. Bathroom / Salle de bains
6. Living room / Salon
7. Covered deck / Galerie couverte

RINCON

Marmol Radziner Prefab
Mobile
© Tyler Boye

The modules, designed and manufactured by Marmol Radziner, are transported already preassembled, reducing the CO_2 emissions. The materials are recycled, such as the steel, or of certified origin, such as wood. The porches and openings create cross ventilation and the glass panes have insulation superior to 39%.

Die von Marmol Radziner entworfenen und hergestellten Module werden bereits montiert angeliefert, wodurch der CO_2-Ausstoß weitgehend reduziert wird. Es werden recycelte Baustoffe (Stahl) und Hölzer mit kontrollierter Herkunft verwendet. Veranden und Fassadenöffnungen sorgen für Kreuzlüftung, die Fenster haben einen 39 % höheren Dämmwert als üblich.

Conçus et fabriqués par Marmol Radziner, les modules sont acheminés déjà montés, ce qui permet de réduire au maximum les émissions de CO_2. Les matériaux sont soit recyclés, comme l'acier, soit de provenance certifiée, comme le bois. Les porches et les ouvertures génèrent une ventilation croisée. Le pouvoir isolant des vitrages est de 39 % supérieur à celui des verres ordinaires.

De modules, die door Marmol Radziner zijn ontworpen en gefabriceerd, zijn voorgemonteerd vervoerd, waardoor de CO_2-uitstoot tot een minimum wordt beperkt. De materialen zijn gerecycled, zoals het staal, ofwel zijn voorzien van een certificaat, in het geval van het hout. De arcades en de openingen zorgen voor kruisventilatie en de ramen bieden 39% meer isolatie.

Los módulos, diseñados y fabricados por Marmol Radziner, se trasladan ya montados, con lo que se reduce al máximo la emisión de CO_2. Los materiales son reciclados, como el acero, o de origen certificado, como la madera. Los porches y las aberturas generan ventilación cruzada y los cristales tienen un aislamiento un 39% superior.

I moduli, progettati e realizzati da Marmol Radziner, vengono trasportati già montati riducendo al massimo le emissioni di CO_2. I materiali sono riciclati come l'acciaio o di origine certificata come il legno. I porticati e le aperture creano una ventilazione incrociata e i vetri hanno un isolamento superiore del 39%.

Os módulos, projectados e fabricados pela Marmol Radziner, são transportados já montados, com o que se reduz ao máximo a emissão de CO_2. Os materiais são reciclados, como o aço, ou de origem certificada, como a madeira. Os alpendres e as aberturas geram ventilação cruzada e os vidros permitem um maior isolamento, em cerca de 39%.

3D rendering / Représentation en 3D

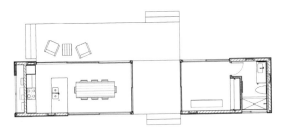

Floor plan / Rez-de-chaussée

ENGLISH RESIDENCE

ZeroEnergy Design
Orleans, MA, USA
© ZeroEnergy Design

The renovation of this 1958 home allowed the architects, specialists in green building, to incorporate a few energy saving measures: the radiant heating stabilizes the temperature throughout the house, the wood is origin controlled and solar panels have been installed, which provide clean energy.

Beim Umbau dieses Wohnhauses aus dem Jahre 1958 konnten die auf nachhaltiges Bauen spezialisierten Architekten einige Energiesparmaßnahmen umsetzen: Die Fußbodenheizung stabilisiert die Raumtemperatur im gesamten Haus, das Holz stammt aus kontrollierter Forstwirtschaft und die installierten Sonnenkollektoren erzeugen sauberen Strom.

La rénovation de cette villa de 1958 a permis aux architectes, spécialisés en constructions durables, de recourir à des solutions favorisant les économies d'énergie : le chauffage radiant assure une température égale dans toute la maison, le bois provient de forêt gérées et les panneaux solaires fournissent une énergie propre.

Door deze woning uit 1958 te renoveren konden de architecten, gespecialiseerd in duurzame constructies, enkele maatregelen voor energiebesparing invoeren: stralingsverwarming waarmee de temperatuur in het hele huis wordt gestabiliseerd, hout van gecontroleerde oorsprong en zonnepanelen die schone energie leveren.

La renovación de esta residencia de 1958 permitió a los arquitectos, especializados en construcciones sostenibles, incorporar algunas medidas para el ahorro energético: la calefacción radiante estabiliza la temperatura en toda la casa, la madera es de origen controlado y se han incorporado paneles solares, que proporcionan energía limpia.

La ristrutturazione di questa abitazione del 1958 ha consentito agli architetti - specializzati in edilizia sostenibile - di applicare alcune misure volte al risparmio energetico: il riscaldamento radiante stabilizza la temperatura in tutta la casa, il legno è di origine controllata e sono stati installati alcuni pannelli solari per la produzione di energia pulita.

A renovação desta casa de 1958 permitiu aos arquitectos, especializados em construções sustentáveis, incorporar algumas medidas para a poupança energética: o aquecimento radiante estabiliza a temperatura em toda a casa, a madeira é de origem controlada e foram incorporados painéis solares, que produzem energia limpa.

Ground floor / Rez-de-chaussée

Second floor / Premier étage

1. Bedroom / Chambre
2. Bathroom / Salle de bains
3. Laundry / Buanderie
4. Kitchen / Cuisine
5. Living room / Salon
6. Dining room / Salle à manger
7. Covered porch / Porche couvert
8. TV room / Salle télé
9. Study / Bureau
10. Outdoor kitchen / Cuisine extérieure
11. Terrace / Terrasse
12. Green roof / Couverture végétale

ALPINE HUT

Ofis Arhitekti
Podpeč, Slovenia
© Tomaz Gregoric

This cabin, located in a natural park, follows a strict building regulation. The original dimensions were maintained but with changes to improve the energy efficiency. The central chimney heats the two floors and the glass and thermal mass complete the air conditioning. Rainwater is collected for reuse.

Beim Bau dieser in einem Naturpark gelegenen Hütte wurden die ursprünglichen Abmessungen beibehalten und die Energieeffizienz wurde gesteigert. Der zentrale Kamin heizt beide Etagen. Abgerundet wird der Bereich Klimatisierung durch die Verglasung und den Einsatz wärmespeichernder Materialien. Regenwasser wird für die Wiederverwendung aufgefangen.

Ce refuge, dans un parc naturel, est construit selon des normes très strictes. La rénovation n'a pas modifié les dimensions d'origine mais les changements apportés ont considérablement amélioré son efficacité énergétique. La cheminée centrale chauffe les deux étages. Le vitrage et la masse thermique complètent la climatisation. Les eaux de pluie sont collectées.

Deze hut, gelegen in een natuurpark, voldoet aan de zeer strenge bouwregels. De originele dimensies zijn behouden, maar er zijn wijzigingen ingevoerd om de energie-efficiëntie te verbeteren. De centrale open haard verwarmt de twee verdiepingen en de luchtbehandeling wordt verbeterd door het glas en thermische massa. Het regenwater wordt opgevangen en kan opnieuw worden gebruikt.

Esta cabaña, situada en un parque natural, sigue una normativa de edificación muy estricta. Se mantuvieron las dimensiones originales pero con cambios para mejorar la eficacia energética. La chimenea central calienta las dos plantas y el cristal y la masa térmica completan la climatización. El agua de la lluvia se recoge para su reutilización.

Questa capanna situata in un parco naturale segue una normativa edilizia molto rigida. Sono state mantenute le dimensioni originarie applicando però delle modifiche per migliorare l'efficienza energetica. Il camino centrale riscalda i due piani mentre i vetri e la massa termica completano la climatizzazione. L'acqua piovana viene raccolta per essere poi riutilizzata.

Esta cabana, situada num parque natural, cumpre uma norma de edificação muito restritiva. Mantiveram-se as dimensões originais, mas com alterações para melhorar a eficácia energética. A chaminé central aquece os dois pisos e o vidro e a massa térmica completam a climatização. A água da chuva é recolhida para reutilização.

Photomontage of location / Photomontage de l'implantation

Site plan / Plan de la parcelle

1 : 1

Cross section / Coupe transversale

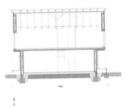

2
2

Longitudinal section / Coupe longitudinale

Elevations / Élévations

Alteration of the facade / Modification de la façade

Ground floor / Rez-de-chaussée

Second floor / Premier étage

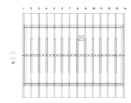

Roof plan / Toiture en terrasse couverte

Construction details: isolation / Détail de la construction : isolation

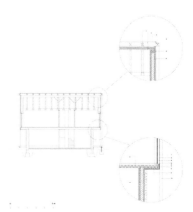

BETWEEN ALDER AND OAK

Andreas Wenning/Baumraum
Bad Rothenfelde, Germany
© Alasdair Jardine

This cabin is an example of a lightweight ecological construction. The durability of these buildings largely depends on the life span of the tree. In this case, oak has been used as the main construction material both on the exterior and interior. The handrails are made from wood and steel and stone wool has been used as insulation.

Dies ist ein Beispiel für ökologisches und leichtgewichtiges Bauen. Die Lebensdauer dieser Häuser hängt in großem Maße von der Lebensdauer des Baumes ab, in dem sie errichtet werden. Hier wurde innen und außen größtenteils Eichenholz verbaut. Die Geländer wurden aus Holz und Stahl gefertigt, für die Isolierung wurde Steinwolle verwendet.

Cette cabane fournit un bon exemple de construction écologique légère. L'espérance de vie de ce type de construction dépend en grande partie de celle de l'arbre qui les accueille. C'est ici le chêne qui domine, autant pour l'extérieur que l'intérieur. Les rambardes sont en bois et acier et l'isolation en laine de roche.

Deze hut is een voorbeeld van lichte ecologische bouw. De duurzaamheid van deze constructies is in grote mate afhankelijk van de levensduur van de boom waarin ze gebouwd zijn. In dit geval is eikenhout, zowel binnen als buiten, het belangrijkste bouwmateriaal. De balustrades zijn van hout en staal en de isolatie van steenwol.

Esta cabaña es un ejemplo de construcción ecológica de estructura ligera. La durabilidad de estas edificaciones depende en gran medida de la vida del árbol que las acoge. En este caso, el roble es el material constructivo predominante tanto en el exterior como en el interior. Las barandillas son de madera y acero y el aislamiento es de lana de roca.

Questa capanna è un esempio di edificio ecologico dalla struttura leggera. La durata di queste unità dipende in gran parte dalla vita dell'albero che le accoglie. In questo caso il rovere è il materiale costruttivo predominante sia all'esterno che all'interno. Le ringhiere di protezione sono in legno e acciaio; l'isolamento è garantito con l'impiego di lana di roccia.

Esta cabana é um exemplo de construção ecológica de estrutura leve. A durabilidade destas edificações depende em grande medida da vida da árvore que as acolhe. Neste caso, o carvalho é o material de construção predominante tanto no exterior como no interior. Os varandins são de madeira e aço e o isolamento é de lã de rocha.

Cross section / Élévation transversale

Longitudinal section / Élévation longitudinale

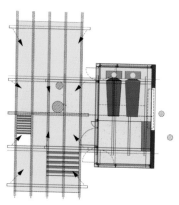

Terrace floor plan / Terrasse

MOUNTAIN RESEARCH

Shin Ohori, Setaro Aso/General Design
Kawakami-mura, Nagano, Japan
© Daici Ano

Local pine has been primarily used in this home. Solar panels provide the energy that converts sunlight into electricity and thermal panels heat the water. Finally, the design of the rooms seeks to make best use of sunlight to reduce the energy consumption.

Bei diesem Wohnhaus wurde im Wesentlichen Holz lokaler Kiefern verbaut. Photovoltaikpaneele verwandeln das Sonnenlicht in elektrische Energie, das Wasser wird mithilfe von Wärmekollektoren erhitzt. Beim Design der einzelnen Räume wurde darauf geachtet, das Sonnenlicht optimal auszunutzen, um den Energieverbrauch zu senken.

Le pin d'origine locale est le principal matériau de construction. L'énergie est fournie par les panneaux solaires qui convertissent la lumière du soleil en électricité. L'eau est chauffée par les panneaux thermiques. Le plan des bungalows exploite au maximum la lumière du jour pour réduire la consommation d'énergie.

In deze woning is met name plaatselijk grenenhout gebruikt. De energie wordt geleverd door zonnepanelen die zonlicht omzetten in elektriciteit en het water wordt met thermische panelen verwarmd. Tenslotte is het ontwerp van de vertrekken erop gericht om maximaal profijt te trekken uit zonlicht, om het energieverbruik terug te dringen.

En esta residencia se ha utilizado principalmente madera de pino local. La energía la proporcionan paneles solares, que convierten la luz del sol en electricidad, y el agua se calienta con paneles térmicos. Por último, el diseño de las estancias busca aprovechar al máximo la luz solar para reducir el consumo energético.

In questo edificio è stato utilizzato principalmente legno di pino locale. L'energia è garantita da alcuni pannelli solari che trasformano la luce del sole in elettricità mentre l'acqua viene riscaldata con i pannelli termici. Infine, il progetto degli ambienti interni mira a sfruttare al massimo la luce solare per ridurre il consumo energetico.

Nesta habitação foi utilizada principalmente madeira de pinho local. A energia é proporcionada por painéis solares, que convertem a luz do sol em electricidade, e a água é aquecida por painéis térmicos. Por último, o design das divisões procura aproveitar ao máximo a luz solar para reduzir o consumo energético.

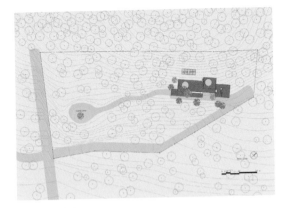

Site plan / Plan de situation

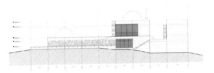

Elevation / Élévation

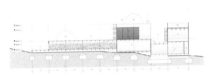

Longitudinal section / Coupe longitudinale

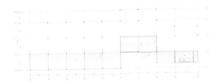

Ground floor / Rez-de-chaussée

Longitudinal section / Coupe longitudinale

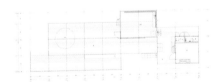

Second floor / Premier étage

Cross section / Coupe transversale

WOODY 85

Marianne Borge
Drøbak, Norway
© Ivan Brodey

The starting point for this 35 m² (376.7 ft²) cabin is sustainable design and savings resources. The height and breadth of the space and the large glass wall seek to achieve comfort and the entry of light. Wood that does not require maintenance is the main material used. A single biomass stove is enough to heat the interior.

Diese Hütte mit einer Fläche von nur 35 m² basiert auf nachhaltigem Design und der Einsparung von Ressourcen. Die Höhe und Weite des Baus sowie die großflächige Glaswand zielen auf hohen Komfort und viel Tageslichteinfall ab. Hölzer ohne Instandhaltungsaufwand sind die hier verwendeten grundlegenden Baustoffe. Bereits ein einziger Biomasseofen reicht aus, um das gesamte Haus zu beheizen.

Cette maisonnette, dont la surface ne dépasse pas 35 m², est l'aboutissement d'un plan durable favorisant l'économie des ressources. La hauteur et l'amplitude de l'ensemble ainsi qu'une grande baie vitrée donnent une impression d'espace et favorise l'entrée de la lumière. Le bois, qui n'exige aucun entretien particulier, est le matériau principal. Un unique foyer à biomasse suffit à chauffer tout l'intérieur.

De uitgangspunten van deze hut van slechts 35 m² zijn het duurzame ontwerp en de besparing van natuurlijke hulpbronnen. De hoogte en de omvang van het geheel en de grote glazen muur zorgen voor meer comfort en lichtinval. Het onderhoudsvrije hout is het belangrijkste materiaal. Er is maar een biomassakachel nodig om de hut van binnen te verwarmen.

El punto de partida de esta cabaña de solo 35 m² es el diseño sostenible y el ahorro de recursos. La altura y la amplitud del conjunto y la gran pared de cristal persiguen el confort y la entrada de luz. La madera, que no requiere mantenimiento, es el material principal. Una única estufa de biomasa es suficiente para calentar el interior.

Il punto di partenza di questa capanna di appena 35 m² è il progetto sostenibile e il risparmio di risorse. L'altezza e l'ampiezza della struttura e la grande parete di vetro garantiscono il comfort e l'ingresso di luce. Il legno, che non richiede manutenzione, è il materiale principale. Un'unica stufa a biomassa basta per riscaldare l'ambiente interno.

O ponto de partida desta cabana de apenas 35 m² é o design sustentável e a poupança de recursos. A altura e a amplitude do conjunto e a grande parede de vidro procuram o conforto e a entrada de luz. A madeira, que não requer manutenção, é o material principal. Um único fogão de sala biomassa é suficiente para aquecer o interior.

KONA RESIDENCE

Belzberg Architects
Kona, Hawaii
© Benny Chan (Fotoworks), Belzberg Architects

The sustainability strategies of the house maintain balance with the natural environment. Separated from the house, a few photovoltaic panels provide electricity. The volcanic rock helps to heat the pool water and rainwater is collected and reused in the gardens. Some materials, such as the wooden exterior, are recycled.

Die bei diesem Haus umgesetzten Nachhaltigkeitsstrategien halten das Gleichgewicht mit der natürlichen Umgebung aufrecht. Einige in der Nähe des Hauses installierte Photovoltaikpaneele erzeugen elektrische Energie. Das Vulkangestein erwärmt das Wasser im Swimmingpool, das Regenwasser wird aufgefangen und für die Bewässerung des Gartens. Bei einigen Baustoffe, wie z. B. beim Holz für den Außenbereich, handelt es sich um Recyclingmaterialien.

Les stratégies de développement durable mises en œuvre pour cette propriété ont permis le maintien de l'équilibre avec le milieu naturel. Indépendants de la maison, les panneaux photovoltaïques fournissent l'énergie électrique. La roche volcanique contribue au chauffage de l'eau de la piscine ; les eaux pluviales récupérées sont utilisées pour l'arrosage des terrasses. Certains matériaux, comme le bois de l'habillage extérieur, sont recyclés.

De strategieën van duurzaamheid van het huis houden het evenwicht met de omgeving in stand. Enkele fotovoltaïsche zonnepanelen, die los van het huis staan, leveren de elektrische energie. De vulkanische rotsgrond helpt om het water van het zwembad te verwarmen en regenwater wordt opgevangen om de als tuin aangelegde zones te bevloeien. Enkele materialen, zoals het hout aan de buitenkant, zijn gerecycled.

Las estrategias de sostenibilidad de esta vivienda mantienen el equilibrio con el entorno natural. Separadas de la casa, unas placas fotovoltaicas proporcionan energía eléctrica. La roca volcánica ayuda a calentar el agua de la piscina y el agua de la lluvia se recoge y reutiliza en las zonas ajardinadas. Algunos materiales, como la madera exterior, son reciclados.

Le strategie di sostenibilità della casa mantengono l'equilibrio con l'ambiente naturale. Separati dalla casa, alcuni pannelli fotovoltaici forniscono energia elettrica. La roccia vulcanica contribuisce a riscaldare l'acqua della piscina mentre l'acqua piovana viene raccolta e riutilizzata nelle zone verdi. Alcuni materiali come il legno esterno sono riciclati.

As estratégias de sustentabilidade da casa mantêm o equilíbrio com o meio natural. Separadas da casa, painéis fotovoltaicos proporcionam energia eléctrica. A rocha vulcânica ajuda a aquecer a água da piscina e a água da chuva é recolhida e reutilizada nas zonas ajardinadas. Alguns materiais, como a madeira exterior, são reciclados.

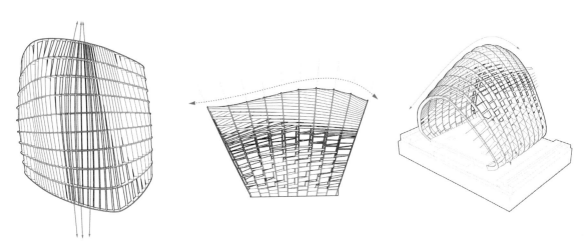

Axonometrics of the entry pavilion / Axonométries du pavillon de l'entrée

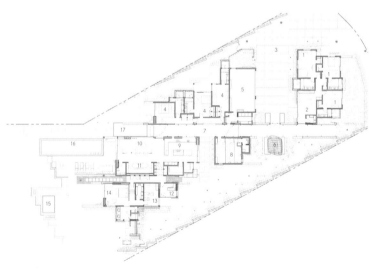

1. Kid's room / Chambre d'enfant
2. Kid's common / Salle de jeux
3. Motor court / Patio entrée
4. Guest room / Chambre d'amis
5. Garage / Garage
6. Entry pavilion / Pavillon entrée
7. Outdoor gallery / Galerie extérieure
8. Theater / Salle de projection
9. Kitchen / Cuisine
10. Great room / Salon principal
11. Dining room / Salle à manger
12. Study / Bureau
13. Gym / Salle de gym
14. Master bedroom / Chambre principale
15. Hot tub / Jacuzzi
16. Pool / Piscine
17. Reflecting pool / Bassin

Floor plan / Étage

BRUNSELL-SHARPLES HOUSE

Obie G. Bowman
The Sea Ranch, CA, USA
© Obie G. Bowman, Robert Foothrap

Construction in favor of nature is one of the premises of the work by Obie G. Bowman. This home contains several strategies that seek the balance between architecture and the environment. The green roof insulates the interior and its inclination protects it from the wind. The majority of the material is recycled and the openings improve ventilation and lighting.

Obie G. Bowman verfolgt das Ziel, im Einklang mit der Natur zu bauen. Bei diesem Wohnhaus aus größtenteils recycelten Materialien wurde versucht, Architektur und Umwelt ins Gleichgewicht zu bringen. Die Neigung des als Wärmedämmung dienenden bepflanzten Dachs schützt vor dem Wind. Die Fassadenöffnungen verbessern Belüftung und Tageslichteinfall.

Construire en symbiose avec la nature est l'un des fondements de l'œuvre de Obie G. Bowman. Cette résidence associe plusieurs stratégies visant à instaurer un équilibre entre l'architecture et le milieu naturel. La toiture végétale isole l'intérieur et la pente du toit protège du vent. Une grande partie des matériaux est recyclée et les ouvertures améliorent la ventilation et l'éclairage.

Milieuvriendelijk bouwen is een van de premisses van het werk van Obie G. Bowman. In deze woning zijn verschillende strategieën gebruikt, waarbij gezocht is naar een evenwicht tussen architectuur en de natuurlijke omgeving. Het dak isoleert het interieur en het afschot beschermt tegen de wind. Het materiaal is grotendeels gerecycled en de openingen verbeteren de ventilatie en verlichting.

Construir respetando la naturaleza es una de las premisas de la obra de Obie G. Bowman. Esta residencia reúne varias estrategias que buscan el equilibrio entre la arquitectura y el medio natural. La cubierta vegetal aísla el interior y su inclinación protege del viento. Gran parte del material es reciclado y las aberturas mejoran la ventilación y la iluminación.

Costruire nel rispetto della natura è una delle premesse del lavoro di Obie G. Bowman. Questa abitazione riunisce varie strategie che ricercano l'equilibrio tra architettura e ambiente. Il rivestimento vegetale isola l'interno e la sua inclinazione protegge dal vento. Gran parte del materiale è riciclato e le aperture migliorano la ventilazione e l'illuminazione.

Construir em favor da natureza é uma das premissas da obra de Obie G. Bowman. Esta residência reúne várias estratégias que procuram o equilíbrio entre a arquitectura e o meio natural. A cobertura vegetal isola o interior e a sua inclinação protege do vento. Grande parte do material é reciclado e as aberturas melhoram a ventilação e a iluminação.

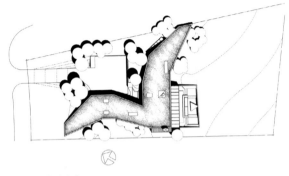

Location plan / Plan de situation

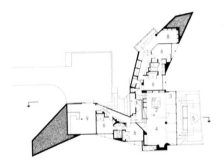

Floor plan / Rez-de-chaussée

1. Entrance / Entrée
2. Kitchen / Cuisine
3. Dining room / Salle à manger
4. Living room / Salon
5. Roof / Toiture

6. Bedroom / Chambre
7. Bathroom / Salle de bains
8. Study / Bureau
9. Shop – Garage / Boutique – Garage

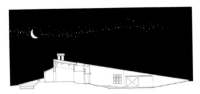

Section / Coupe

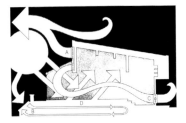

Bioclimatic diagram / Diagramme bioclimatique

A. Continuous discharge manifold / Échange en continu
B. Solar hot water collector / Collecteur solaire d'eau chaude
C. Air intake louvers / Grille de prise d'air
D. Brick over slab floor mass / Sol en brique posée sur une dalle

RECYCLED MATERIALS CABIN

Juan Luis Martínez Nahuel
Comuna de Panguipulli, Chile
© Juan Luis Martínez Nahuel

The unique feature of this refuge is that the construction materials are reused. The lot, which is difficult to access, also meant that modular construction was required. These characteristics achieve a major reduction in CO_2 and in the environmental impact as the construction time is reduced.

Für den Bau dieser besonderen Hütte kamen wiederverwendete Materialen zum Einsatz. Der schwierige Zugang zum Grundstück bedingte die verwendete modulare Bauweise. Beide Merkmale sorgen für eine erhebliche Senkung des CO_2-Ausstoßes und der Umweltbelastung (durch die Verkürzung der Bauzeit).

Tous les matériaux utilisés pour ce remarquable refuge proviennent de constructions antérieures. La difficulté d'accès à la parcelle a favorisé le choix d'une construction modulaire. L'association de ces deux options aboutit à une importante réduction des émissions de CO_2, puisque l'impact des matériaux sur le milieu est réduit et la durée du chantier écourtée.

Het bijzondere aan deze hut is dat de bouwmaterialen hergebruikt zijn. De moeilijke bereikbaarheid van het perceel was ook de reden voor een modulaire constructie. Door deze kenmerken wordt een aanzienlijke vermindering van CO_2 behaald, en er minder impact is op het milieu, doordat de bouwtijd korter is.

La particularidad de este refugio es que todos los materiales de construcción son reutilizados. La dificultad de acceso a la parcela también determinó un tipo de construcción modular. La conjunción de estas estas características ha supuesto una importante reducción de CO_2 y del impacto medioambiental, pues el tiempo de construcción es menor.

La peculiarità di questo rifugio è che i materiali da costruzione sono riutilizzati. La difficoltà di accesso alla proprietà ha portato alla scelta di un tipo di costruzione modulare. Queste caratteristiche consentono di ottenere una forte riduzione delle emissioni di CO_2 e a basso impatto ambientale, con tempi di costruzione ridotti.

A particularidade deste refúgio é que os materiais de construção provêm de reutilização. A dificuldade de acesso à parcela também implicou um tipo de construção modular. Estas características permitem uma importante redução de CO_2 e de baixo impacto ambiental, tendo-se reduzido o tempo de construção.

Sketch / Croquis

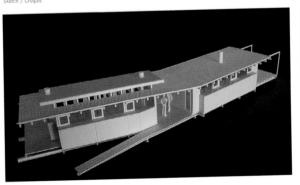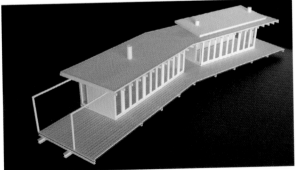

Models / Maquettes

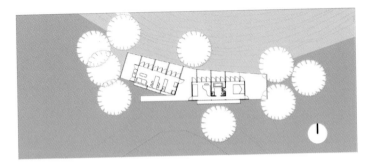

Floor plan / Niveau

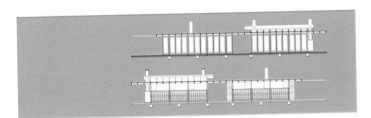

Elevations / Élévations

@6 Architecture
San Francisco, CA, USA
www.at-six.com

+31 Architects
Amsterdam, The Netherlands
www.plus31architects.com

24H Architecture
Rotterdam, The Netherlands
www.24h-architecture.com

Aires Mateus e Associados
Lisboa, Portugal
www.airesmateus.com

Andersson Wise Architects
Austin, TX, USA
www.anderssonwise.com

Andrea Tognon Architecture
Milan, Italy
www.atognon.com

Architekt Kuczia
Osnabrück, Germany
www.kuczia.com

Barton Myers Associates
Los Angeles, CA, USA
www.bartonmyers.com

Baumraum
Bremen, Germany
www.baumraum.de

BDA Architecture
Broadbeaach, QLD, Australia
www.bdaarch.com.au

Belzberg Architects
Santa Monica, CA, USA
www.belzbergarchitects.com

Bercy Chen Studio
Austin, TX, USA
http://bcarc.com

Bligh Voller Nield
Brisbane, QLD, Australia
www.bvn.au

Breathe Architects
Ontario, ON, Canada
www.breathebyassociation.com

Bricault Design
Vancouver, BC, Canada
http://bricault.ca

Cary Bernstein Architect
San Francisco, CA, USA
www.cbstudio.com

CCS Architecture
San Francisco, CA, USA
www.ccs-architecture.com

Choi Ropiha
Manly, NSW, Australia
www.choiropiha.com

Conquest Manufacturing
Altona, MB, Canada
www.conquestmfg.ca

Craig Steely Architecture
San Francisco, CA, USA
http://craigsteely.com

Dust Design Build
Tucson, AZ, USA
www.dustdb.com

Fantastic Norway Architects
Oslo, Norway
www.fantasticnorway.no

Forte, Gimenes & Marcondes Ferraz Arquitetos
Sao Paulo, Brazil
www.fgmf.com.br

Francois Perrin
Los Angeles, CA, USA
http://francoisperrin.com

Garrison Architects
Brooklyn, NY, USA
www.garrisonarchitects.com

House & House Architects
San Francisco, CA, USA
www.houseandhouse.com

Iredale Pedersen Hook Architects
Perth, WA, Australia
www.iredalepedersenhook.com

Jeffrey McKean Architect
New York, NY, USA
www.jeffreymckean.com

Jesse Bornstein Architecture
Santa Monica, CA, USA
www.bornarch.com

Juan Luis Martínez Nahuel
juanluismartineznahuel@gmail.com

Kendle Design Collaborative
Scottsdale, AZ, USA
www.kendledesign.com

Kevin deFreitas Architects
San Diego, CA, USA
www.defreitasarchitects.com

Kyu Sung Woo Architects
Cambridge, MA, USA
www.kswa.com

MacKay-Lyons Sweetapple Architects
Halifax, NS, Canada
www.mlsarchitects.ca

Marcy Wong Donn Logan Architects
Berkeley, CA, USA
www.wonglogan.com

Marianne Borge
Oslo, Norway
http://marianneborge.com

Marmol Radziner Prefab
Los Angeles, CA, USA
www.marmolradzinerprefab.com

Max Pritchard Architect
Glenelg, SA, Australia
www.maxpritchardarchitect.com.au

MCK Architecture & Interiors
Surry Hills, NSW, Australia
www.mckarchitects.com

Michelle Kaufmann Studio
Oakland, CA, USA
http://michellekaufmann.com

Morphosis Architects
Santa Monica, CA, USA
www.morphosis.com

M.P. Johnson Design Studio
Cave Creek, AZ, USA
www.mpjstudio.com

Nota Design International
Singapore, Singapore
www.notionvague.com

Obie G. Bowman
Healdsburg, CA, USA
www.obiebowman.com

Office of Mobile Design by Jennifer Siegal
Venice, CA, USA
www.designmobile.com

Ofis Arhitekti
Ljubljana, Slovenia
www.ofis-a.si

Paul Lukez Architecture
Somerville, MA, USA
www.lukez.com

Peter Cardew Architects
Vancouver, BC, Canada
www.cardew.ca

Pitman Tozer Architects
London, UK
www.pitmantozer.com

Popov Bass Architects
Milsons Point, NSW, Australia
www.popovbass.com.au

Resolution: 4 Architecture
New York, NY, USA
http://res4a.com

Riesco + Rivera Arquitectos Asociados
Santiago, Chile
www.riescoyrivera.cl

Robert Konieczny
Katowice, Poland
www.kwkpromes.pl

Shin Ohori, Setaro Aso/General Design
Tokyo, Japan
www.general-design.net

Simon Winstanley Architects
Castle Douglas, UK
www.candwarch.co.uk

SPG Architects
New York, NY, USA
www.spgarchitects.com

Studio 101 Architects
Geelong, VIC, Australia
www.studio101.com.au

Studio 804
Lawrence, KS, USA
www.studio804.com

Studio B Architects
Aspen, CO, USA
www.studiobarchitects.net

Taalman Koch Architecture
Los Angeles, CA, USA
www.taalmankoch.com

Zsuffa és Kalmár Építész Műterem
Budapest, Hungary
www.zsk.hu